Siege and Reduction of

Fort Pulaski

Brig. Gen. Q. A. Gillmore

The Siege and Reduction of Fort Pulaski
by Brig. Gen. Quincy A. Gillmore

Reprinted from the 1862 edition

Printed in the United States of America

Published by THOMAS PUBLICATIONS
P.O. Box 3031
Gettysburg, PA 17325

ISBN-0-939631-07-5

Photo Credits

Front cover — The breach and ruins in the southeast angle of Fort Pulaski. Courtesy of U.S. Army Military History Institute.

Brigadier General Gillmore by C.D. Fredericks & Co., New York. Courtesy Dean S. Thomas.

Back cover — Aerial view of Fort Pulaski National Monument. Courtesy of Eastern National.

PAPERS ON PRACTICAL ENGINEERING.

No. 8.

OFFICIAL REPORT

TO THE

UNITED STATES ENGINEER DEPARTMENT,

OF THE

SIEGE AND REDUCTION

OF

FORT PULASKI,

GEORGIA,

FEBRUARY, MARCH, AND APRIL, 1862.

BY BRIG.-GEN. Q. A. GILLMORE, U. S. VOLS.,

CAPTAIN OF ENGINEERS U. S. A.

ILLUSTRATED BY MAPS AND ENGRAVED VIEWS.

NEW YORK:

D. VAN NOSTRAND, 192 BROADWAY.

1862.

C. A. ALVORD, STEREOTYPER AND PRINTER.

CONTENTS.

Brigadier General Quincy Adams Gillmore

INTRODUCTION

Most of the noteworthy advances in science and technology have been made in the name of national defense. Indeed, military history is a series of grand experiments. And it is one matter to conduct an experiment in the controlled environment of the laboratory and quite another to face it in the real world. Occasionally, individuals have the opportunity to face it under both conditions. They are the history makers. For thirteen years Quincy Adams Gillmore had a noteworthy career as a military engineer after graduating first in his class (1849) at the United States Military Academy. In Virginia, he was Assistant Engineer in the construction of Forts Monroe and Calhoun. In New York, he commanded the harbor fortifications. In South Carolina, he was Chief Engineer at Port Royal. At Fort Pulaski, Georgia, he conducted his grand experiment and made history.

There, in 1862, two centuries of fortification history, the Age of Vauban, squared off against Gillmore and a new strategy. The new strategy was the rifled cannon. It was true that rifled cannon could inflict severe damage to masonry. But rifled cannon had never been used successfully beyond 600 yards and Fort Pulaski's walls were more than three times that distance. Just five months earlier, Brig. Gen. Robert E. Lee, who helped build the fort in 1829, assured the Confederate defenders that Union artillery would never breach the walls. Gillmore secured the reluctant approval of his commanding officer, Thomas W. Sherman, and began preparations for the siege. Early on the morning of April 10, a mortar shell announced the beginning of the attack. Thirty hours later, Fort Pulaski's southeast angle lay in ruin and the Confederates surrendered. Gillmore's great experiment was a complete success and he went on to become one of the nation's most brilliant military engineers.

Word spread quickly throughout the United States and Europe. The era of masonry forts and smoothbore artillery had come to an end. What you are about to read is a detailed account of that grand experiment written by the very man who engineered it. It is a story of scientific research, technological development and strategy. Above all, it is the personal story of one man's role in our never-ending search for national security.

John W. Beck
Chief of Visitor Services
Fort Pulaski National Monument
April, 1988

The information we learn from books never goes out of style. Unfortunately, the books themselves often do. On behalf of the staff at Fort Pulaski National Monument, I say "Thank you" to Dean Thomas for reprinting this classic for a new generation of military historians.

LIST OF PLATES

GENERAL GILLMORE'S REPORT

TO

GEN. TOTTEN, CHIEF ENGINEER U. S. A.

HEAD QUARTERS U. S. FORCES,
TYBEE AND COCKSPUR ISLANDS, GA., *April 30th*, 1862.

SIR:

I HAVE the honor to submit the following report of operations connected with the siege of Fort Pulaski, which resulted in its capitulation to the United States forces on the 11th inst.

1. This success so fully demonstrates the power and effectiveness of rifled cannon, for breaching at long distances,—at distances indeed hitherto untried, and considered altogether impracticable, thus opening a new era in the use of this most valuable, and comparatively unknown arm of service,—has been obtained with such singularly strict adherence to the details of the project, as originally conceived in December last, and has withal, in the developed results, such an important bearing upon the character of our harbor and frontier defences, that I feel called upon to enter into some details.

2. The transfer to another field of labor of Brigadier-

General T. W. Sherman, lately in command of the forces on this coast,—under whose auspices the project for the reduction of Fort Pulaski was pushed forward to within a few days of its final accomplishment,—renders it proper that this report should refer to the preliminary operations directly connected with the siege.

3. In the capacity of Chief Engineer on General Sherman's staff, I was present with the investing forces under General Viele, when the Savannah River was closed above the fort, by the establishment of the battery on Venus Point, Jones Island, on the night of the 11th February last. I took no part in the erection of the Bird Island battery, opposite Venus Point. These two batteries effectually closed the Savannah River.

4. In the double capacity of engineer and commander of the forces, I was charged with the offensive operations on Tybee Island, where the batteries for the reduction of the work were to be established; and also with the completion of the investment, by the blockade of the Wilmington Narrows and Lazaretto Creek passage.

5. The data for this report will therefore be taken, in a measure, from my private journal, and from official correspondence and orders.

FORT PULASKI.

6. Fort Pulaski is situated on Cockspur Island, Georgia, latitude thirty-two degrees two minutes north, and

longitude three degrees fifty-one minutes west from Washington, at the head of Tybee Roads, commanding both channels of the Savannah River. The position is a very strong one. Cockspur Island is wholly marsh, and is about one mile long and half a mile wide.

7. It is a brick-work of five sides, or faces, including the gorge; casemated on all sides; walls seven and a half feet thick, and twenty-five feet high above high water; mounting one tier of guns in embrasures, and one *en barbette.* The gorge is covered by an earthen outwork (demilune) of bold relief.

8. The main work and demilune are both surrounded and divided by a wet ditch. Around the main work, the ditch is forty-eight feet wide; around the demilune, thirty-two feet.

9. The communication with the exterior is through the gorge into the demilune, over a drawbridge, and then through one face of the demilune, over the demilune ditch, by another drawbridge. The scarp of the demilune, and the entire counterscarp of main work and demilune, are revetted with good brick masonry.

10. At the time of the siege, it contained forty-eight guns, of which twenty bore upon the batteries on Tybee, viz.: five ten-inch columbiads, five eight-inch columbiads, four thirty-two pounders, one twenty-four pounder Blakely rifle, two twelve inch and three ten-inch seacoast mortars. A full armament for the work would be 140 guns.

11. On the 29th of November, I was directed by General Sherman to make an examination of Tybee Island and Fort Pulaski, and to report upon the propriety of occupying and holding that island, and upon the practicability (and, if deemed practicable, the best method) of reducing Fort Pulaski. I reported, on December 1st, that I deemed "the reduction of that work practicable, by batteries of mortars and rifled guns established on Tybee Island;" and entered into some details as regards the position of the batteries, the precautions to be observed in their construction, and the intensity of the fire that should be maintained against the work. The immediate occupation of Big Tybee Island, by at least one regiment, was also recommended. (See Appendix A.)

12. The armament proposed for the several batteries comprised ten ten-inch sea-coast mortars, ten thirteen-inch do., eight heavy rifled guns, eight Columbiads (see Appendix B.).

13. The project set forth in these two communications (Appendices A. and B.) received General Sherman's sanction at once, with some slight modification as to the number and calibre of the mortars to be used, and was forwarded to Washington, and approved there.

14. Information was in due time received, that orders to prepare and forward the ordnance and ordnance stores had been issued.

15. For months therefore, preceding the fall of Pulaski,

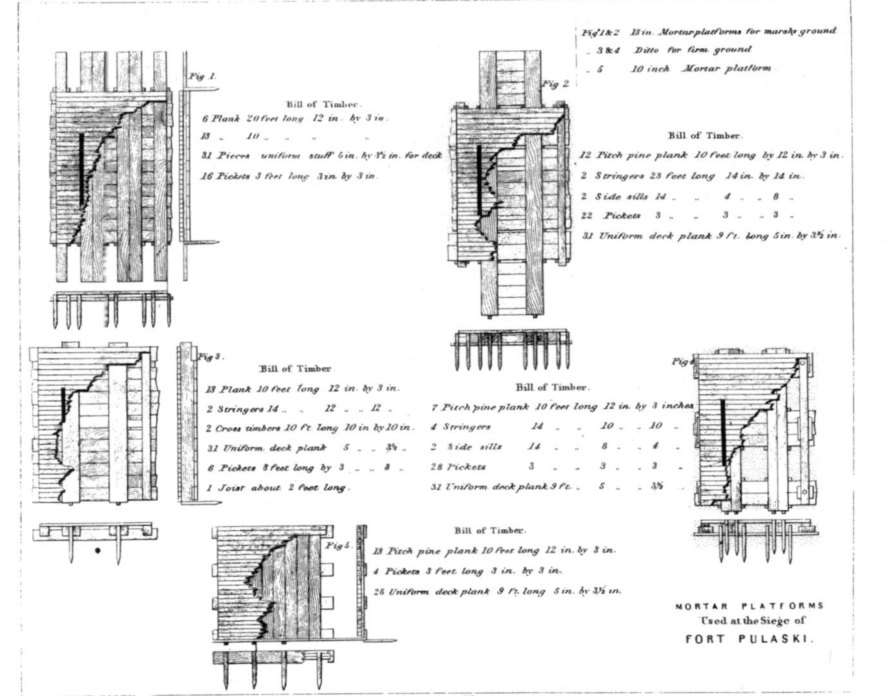

Plate IV. Diagrams of mortar platforms.

Plate V. View of FORT PULASKI and breach, from the South.
A portion of the demilune is seen on the extreme left.

its reduction from Big Tybee, favored by a thorough investment, formed one of General Sherman's approved plans, awaiting only the action of others in sending the necessary supplies for its completion.

16. The 46th regiment New York Volunteers (Colonel R. Rosa) was sent to occupy Big Tybee Island, early in December.

17. Operations for investing the place, by the erection of batteries on the Savannah River, above the work, were set on foot about the middle of January, 1862.

18. It was known to General Sherman before that time, that gunboats of medium draught could enter the river above Fort Pulaski, without encountering any batteries; on the south side through Wassaw Sound, Wilmington Narrows (or Freeborn's Cut), and St. Augustine Creek; and on the north side, through New River, Wall's "Cut," and either Wright or Mud River.

19. Wall's "Cut" is an artificial channel, narrow but deep, connecting New and Wright Rivers, and has for years been used in making the inland water passage between Charleston and Savannah.

20. This "Cut" the enemy had obstructed by an old hulk, and numerous heavy piles, as ascertained about the 1st of January, by Lieutenant J. H. Wilson, Topographical Engineers. These obstructions had all been removed by a detachment of our Engineer troops, under Major Beard, 48th regiment New York volunteers,

secretly sent from Hilton Head by General Sherman for that purpose. The piles were sawed off on a level with the bottom of the stream, and the hulk was swung around against the side of the cut, leaving ample room for the passage of transports and gunboats.

21. The opening of Wall's "Cut," which required four days and four nights to effect, was reported to the Navy on the 14th January, in order that the gunboats might enter the Savannah River, and cover us in the erection of the investing batteries. At this time, the enemy's gunboats were daily passing up and down the river.

22. Mud River is navigable, at high spring tide, for vessels of eight and a half to nine feet draught. Wright River bar has about eleven and a half feet of water at ordinary high tide. The Wright River passage rendered it necessary to approach within about two miles of Fort Pulaski.

23. After the removal of the Wall's Cut obstructions, a joint expedition of land and naval forces, for the investment, was organized by General Sherman and Commodore Dupont.

24. It consisted of one regiment of infantry (the 48th New York volunteers), two companies of the New York volunteer engineers, and two companies of Rhode Island volunteer artillery, with twenty guns of all calibre, viz.: two eight-inch siege howitzers, four thirty-pounder Parrotts, three twenty-pounder Parrotts, three twelve-pounder James, and eight twenty-four-pounder

field howitzers; and was accompanied by three gun boats. The troops were to rendezvous at Daufuskie Island, where we already had three companies of 7th Connecticut volunteers, under Major Gardiner, guarding Wall's "Cut." They had been posted there on January 13th.

25. The land force was in readiness at Hilton Head, soon after the middle of January. Various causes delayed the expected naval co-operation, so that no gunboats passed Wall's "Cut," until the 28th of January.

26. The naval forces were commanded by Commander John Rogers, U. S. N., the land forces by Brigadier-General Viele.

27. Another mixed force, approaching by way of Wassaw Sound, presented itself on the south of the Savannah River, in Wilmington Narrows (or Freeborn's Cut), at the same time, the land force being commanded by Brigadier-General H. G. Wright, and the gunboats by Fleet-Captain Davis.

28. On the afternoon of January 28th, a reconnoissance was made of Mud River, and the Savannah River shore of Jones Island. Venus Point, on the margin of the Savannah, was selected as the position for one of the investing batteries. The line for a road or "causeway," over the marsh between Venus Point and Mud River, was also located. Its length was nearly 1300 yards.

29. Jones Island is nothing but a mud marsh, cov-

ered with reeds and tall grass. The general surface is about on the level of ordinary high tide. There are a few spots of limited area, Venus Point being one of them, that are submerged only by spring tides, or by ordinary tides favored by the wind; but the character of the soil is the same over the whole island. It is a soft, unctuous mud, free of grit or sand, and incapable of supporting a heavy weight. Even in the most elevated places, the partially dry crust is but three or four inches in depth, the substratum being a semi-fluid mud, which is agitated like jelly by the falling of even small bodies upon it, like the jumping of men, or ramming of earth. A pole or an oar can be forced into it with ease, to the depth of twelve or fifteen feet. In most places the resistance diminishes with increase of penetration. Men walking over it are partially sustained by the roots of reeds and grass, and sink in only five or six inches. When this top support gives way, they go down from two to two and one-half feet, and in some places much further.

30. A road or "causeway" of some kind across Jones Island, from Mud River to Venus Point, was deemed necessary, and determined upon at the outset (even if the guns should not have to be carried over it), as the means of getting speedy succor to the Venus Point battery, in case of attack; Daufuskie Island, four miles distant, being the nearest point where troops could be kept for that purpose.

31. On the 29th of January, Lieutenant O'Rorke, of the engineers, was dispatched in a small boat to exam-

ıne Long and Elba Islands, on the Savannah River. Major Beard, 48th New York volunteers, accompanied him. They entered the Savannah river *via* Cunningham Point, at the lower end of Jones Island; pulled up the Savannah, stopping several times on Long and Elba Islands; and went around the west end of the latter, to within about two miles of Fort Jackson.

32. Lieutenant O'Rorke reported the upper end of Long Island favorable for batteries, the surface being fully as high as that at Venus Point.

33. The following extracts from my journal furnish a portion of the history of the operations on Jones Island and the Savannah River, for the investment of Fort Pulaski, and may be properly introduced into this report:

Extracts from Journal of Brigadier-General Gillmore, Chief Engineer Expeditionary Corps.

34. "*February* 1*st*, 2*d*, 3*d*, *and* 4*th*.—The two engineer companies on Daufuskie Island, commanded by Captain Sears, were employed in cutting poles for a 'causeway' on Jones Island, from Mud River to Venus Point, and for the engineer wharf on Daufuskie Island, New River."

35. "On the 4th, the wharf, with eight feet of water at low tide, was completed. 10,000 poles, five to six inches in diameter, and nine feet long, had been cut on Daufuskie Island, and 1,900 of them deposited at the wharf. The men of the 48th New York and 7th Connecticut volunteers transported the poles on their shoul-

ders, the average distance carried being one mile. At the suggestion of Captain Sears, I had a swath cut and cleared of reeds and grass across the upper end of Jones Island, to prevent the enemy burning the island over."

36. "Navy officers were engaged in sounding Mud and Wright rivers. No certainty as yet that the gunboats will enter the Savannah River. Mud River has about one and one-half feet of water in it at extreme low tide, with a very soft, almost semi-fluid bottom. Soundings in Wright River are not completed yet."

37. "*February 5th and 6th.*—Nothing specially new. Engineer force engaged in cutting poles, filling sand-bags on Daufuskie Island, building a temporary wharf of poles and sand-bags on Mud River, and constructing a wheelbarrow track of planks laid end to end, from Venus Point to Mud River wharf. The 48th New York, 7th Connecticut volunteers, and a portion of the engineer forces, engaged in transporting poles and planks, and carrying filled sand-bags from Daufuskie Island to Jones Island (a distance of about four miles) in row boats."

38. "*February 7th and 8th.*—Finished temporary wharf on Mud River; carried several hundred filled sand-bags across to Venus Point; also, a quantity of planks and other battery materials. Had the balance of the engineer materials, required for the Venus Point battery, put into lighters, so as to be ready whenever the gunboats should move. There appears to be no immediate prospect of their moving."

39. "*February 9th.*—I visited Commander Rodgers, to consult in regard to his moving into the Savannah. He said he intended to attempt the Mud River passage that night, on the high tide. The signal of his starting would be one note from his steam-whistle. Returned to Daufuskie, and consulted with General Viele and Captain Hamilton, the Chief of Artillery. It was arranged that the flats, with the guns and ammunition on them, should be towed by the steamer Mayflower, through Wall's Cut, and up Mud River into the Savannah, just behind the gunboats. They were accordingly taken in tow in the evening after dark, from the engineer wharf. The night was windy, rainy, and very dark. The Mayflower, after several attempts, failed to reach Wall's Cut, and cast anchor near the spot she started from. The gunboats did not move, on account of the weather."

40. "*February 10th.*—The gunboats Pembina and Unadilla are at anchor in Wright River, near Wall's Cut. The gunboat Hale has taken up a position in Mud River, about two hundred yards to the eastward of the temporary wharf, in order to protect the landing, and cover us, if driven back. Captain Hamilton quite ill from last night's exposure in the Mayflower. I consulted with General Viele in the afternoon, and it was determined to establish the Venus Point battery at once, and wait no longer for the gunboats to go ahead of us;* also, to effect this by landing the guns on Jones Island, from Mud River, and hauling them over the marsh, in-

* Orders from General Sherman to that effect were subsequently received that same evening.

2

stead of towing them into the Savannah in flats, as first contemplated. Major Beard, 48th New York Volunteers, and Lieutenant J. H. Wilson, Topographical Engineers, volunteered to assist Lieutenant Horace Porter, the ordnance officer, in getting the flats into Mud River, and the guns on shore and into position. Accordingly, the flats with the guns were towed by our row-boats up the river, against the tide, and landed without accident. Two of them were taken about three hundred yards into the marsh, by Lieutenant Wilson. The 48th New York Volunteers furnished the fatigue parties, which had already been twenty-four hours at work on Jones Island, and were very much exhausted. Deeming it impossible to get the guns over that night, I directed them to be covered with reeds and grass, to prevent their discovery by the enemy, and left there until the following night."

41. "During the night of the 10th, Lieutenant O'Rorke of the Engineers, with a party of volunteer engineers, commenced the magazine and gun platforms at Venus Point. The party concealed their work at daybreak (11th), and withdrew. The platforms were made by raising the surface five or six inches, with sand carried over in bags. On this sand foundation, thick planks, perpendicular to the line of the battery, were laid, nearly but not quite in contact with each other. At right angles to these, deck-planks were laid, giving a platform nine by seventeen feet. The floor of the magazine was twenty inches above the natural surface, and rested on sand-bags."

42. "*February* 11*th*.—Continued getting battery and road materials to Jones Island during the day. Early in the evening I went to Jones Island, with fresh men, to finish the labor of getting the guns over. Lieutenants Wilson and Porter and Major Beard took charge of the fatigue parties, as before. The work was done in the following manner: The pieces, mounted on their carriages and limbered up, were moved forward on shifting runways of planks (about fifteen feet long, one foot wide, and three inches thick), laid end to end. Lieutenant Wilson, with a party of thirty-five men, took charge of the two pieces in advance (an eight-inch siege howitzer and a thirty-pounder Parrott), and Major Beard and Lieutenant Porter, with a somewhat larger force, of the four pieces in the rear (two twenty and two thirty-pounder Parrotts). Each party had one pair of planks in excess of the number required for the guns and limbers to rest upon, when closed together. This extra pair of planks being placed in front, in prolongation of those already under the carriages, the pieces were then drawn forward with drag-ropes, one after the other, the length of a plank, thus freeing the two planks in the rear, which, in their turn, were carried to the front. This labor is of the most fatiguing kind. In most places the men sank to their knees in the mud; in some places, much deeper. This mud being of the most slippery and slimy kind, and perfectly free from grit and sand, the planks soon became entirely smeared over with it. Many delays and much exhausting labor were occasioned by the gun-carriages slipping off the planks. When this occurred, the wheels would suddenly sink to the hubs, and powerful levers had to be devised to raise

them up again. I authorized the men to encase their feet in sand-bags, to keep the mud out of their shoes. Many did this, tying the strings just below the knees. The magazines and platforms were ready for service at daybreak. Lieutenant Wilson got his two pieces into position at half-past 2 A. M., and Major Beard and Lieutenant Porter, their four pieces at half-past 8 A. M., on the 12th. At 3 A. M., Lieutenant Wilson started back to General Viele, on Daufuskie, to report the success."

43. "*February* 12*th*.—After giving directions for the fresh relief to be put to work in throwing up a dike around the battery, to keep out the spring tides, which were beginning to flow, I returned to Daufuskie Island.

"The high tide to-day came within eight inches of the surface at Venus Point."

44. "*February* 13*th*, 14*th*, *and* 15*th*.—Various causes, particularly the weather, delayed the establishment of the battery on Long Island."

45. "On the morning of the 13th, the rebel steamer *Ida* passed down by Venus Point, under full steam. Nine shots were fired at her, striking astern, all but one. Elevation good, but not enough allowance made for speed of vessel. I was not in the battery at the time. All the pieces, except one thirty-pounder, recoiled off the platforms. These were at once enlarged to eighteen feet by seventeen and a half feet."

46. "On the afternoon of the 14th, three rebel gunboats came down the river, and opened fire on the bat-

tery, taking a position about one mile distant. Battery fired about thirty shots. One of the vessels was struck. The boats then withdrew."

47. "*February* 16*th.*—The steamer *Ida*, which ran the battery on the 13th, left Fort Pulaski and returned to Savannah, *via* Lazaretto Creek, Wilmington Narrows, Turner's Creek, and St. Augustine Creek."

48. "*February* 17*th.*—I returned to Hilton Head, by General Sherman's order, leaving Lieutenant O'Rorke with General Viele, with written instructions concerning the engineering operations to be carried on."

49. The foregoing extracts from my Journal, are all that bear directly upon the operations on the Savannah above Fort Pulaski.

50. I did not return there on duty. I soon received official information, however, that a second battery, consisting of one eight-inch siege howitzer, one thirty-pounder Parrott, one twenty-pounder Parrott, and three twelve-pounder James, was established on Bird Island, just above Long Island. This was done on the night of February 20th, the flats, with the guns, ammunition, &c., on them, being towed up Mud River, and across the Savannah, by row-boats. Lieutenant O'Rorke of the engineers was present as engineer officer, and Lieutenant Porter as ordnance officer; Captain John Hamilton, General Sherman's chief of artillery, was also present.

51. On the 19th of February, I was ordered to Big

Tybee Island, to place it "in a thorough state of defence against approach from Wilmington Narrows and Lazaretto Creek, to prevent all approach by water, and blockade the channel," thereby completing the investments, and also to "commence operations for the bombardment of Fort Pulaski."

52. The absolute blockade of Pulaski dates from the 22d of February, at which time I stationed two companies of the 46th N. Y. Volunteers, with a battery of two field-pieces, on Decent Island, Lazaretto Creek. This force was subsequently placed on board an old hulk, anchored in Lazaretto Creek, about two and a quarter miles from Fort Pulaski. One thirty-pounder Parrott was then added to the battery. A small guard-boat, mounting a navy six-pounder, was posted considerably in advance of the hulk, to intercept messengers attempting to reach Fort Pulaski by way of McQueen's Island marsh. On the 31st of March, the guard-boat and eighteen men were captured by a large scouting party of the enemy, who suddenly appeared on Wilmington Island. After this the services of the gunboat Norwich, Captain Duncan, were secured in Wilmington Narrows, to assist the blockade.

53. It was found impossible to perfectly isolate the work. In order to appreciate the difficulty, and even impracticability of securing, with ordinary means, the complete blockade of a place like Fort Pulaski, it is necessary to understand something of the topography of the position.

54. The Savannah River, from its mouth on Tybee Roads, to its confluence with St. Augustine Creek, eight miles above, is skirted on both sides by low marsh islands, submerged by spring tides, covered with a thick growth of reeds and tall grass, and cut up by numerous small tortuous creeks and bayous. With light boats that can be hauled over the marsh by hand, from creek to creek, small parties, familiar with the locality, can, with comparative security, find their way over these marshes, in the night, and avoid guards and pickets. It was known that messengers passed to and from the fort, in this way, quite frequently. Several of these were caught. One of them started from the fort and made his escape to Savannah, just after the white flag was raised, on the day of the surrender.

55. On the 21st of February, the first vessel with ordnance and ordnance stores for the siege, arrived in Tybee Roads. From that time until the 9th of April, all the troops on Tybee Island, consisting of the seventh regiment Connecticut Volunteers, the forty-sixth regiment New York Volunteers, two companies of the Volunteer Engineers, and, for the most of the time, two companies third Rhode Island Volunteer Artillery, were constantly engaged in landing and transporting ordnance, ordnance stores, and battery materials, making fascines and roads, constructing gun and mortar batteries, service and dépôt magazines, splinter and bomb-proof shelters for the reliefs of cannoniers off duty, and drilling at the several pieces.

56. The armament comprised thirty-six pieces, dis-

tributed in eleven batteries, at various distances from the fort, as shown in the following table:

1.	Battery,	Stanton,	3	heavy 13-inch Mortars,	at 3,400 yds.
2.	"	Grant,	3	" " " "	" 3,200 "
3.	"	Lyon,	3	" 10 " Columbiads,	" 3,100 "
4.	"	Lincoln,	3	" 8 " "	" 3,045 "
5.	"	Burnside,	1	heavy 13 " Mortar,	" 2,750 "
6.	"	Sherman,	3	" " " "	" 2,650 "
7.	"	Halleck,	2	" " " "	" 2,400 "
8.	"	Scott,	3 1	10-in. 8-in. } Columbiads, "	" 1,740 "
9.	"	Sigel,	5 1	30-p'dr. Parrott, 48 " James, (old 24 p'dr.)	" 1,670 "
10.	"	McClellan,	2 2	84 " " (" 42 ") 64 " " (" 32 ")	" 1,650 "
11.	"	Totten	4	10-inch Siege Mortars,	" 1,650 "

57. Each battery had a service magazine capable of containing a supply of powder for about two days' firing. A dépôt powder magazine, of 3,600 barrels capacity, was constructed near the Martello Tower, which was the landing-place for all the supplies.

58. For a description of the manner of unloading the heavy ordnance upon an exposed beach,—remarkable for its heavy surf,—and of the means adopted for transporting it, by the labor of men exclusively, over a swampy and unsafe road, to the several batteries, located at points varying from one mile to two and a half miles from the landing-place, I refer you to the report of Lieutenant Horace Porter, chief of ordnance and artilery, hereunto appended.

59. Serious difficulties were encountered in making a road sufficiently firm to serve for this heavy transportation.

60. Tybee Island is mostly a mud marsh, like other marsh islands on this coast. Several ridges and hummocks of firm ground, however, exist upon it, and the shore of Tybee Roads, where the batteries were located, is partially skirted by low sand-banks, formed by the gradual and protracted action of the wind and tides. The distance along this shore, from the landing-place to the advanced batteries, is about two and a half miles. The last mile of this route, on which the seven most advanced batteries were placed, is low and marshy, lies in full view of Fort Pulaski, and is within effective range of its guns. The construction of a causeway, resting on fascines and brushwood, over this swampy portion of the line; the erection of the several batteries, with the magazines, gun platforms, and splinter-proof shelters; the transportation of the heaviest ordnance in our service, by the labor of men alone; the hauling of ordnance stores and engineer supplies, and the mounting of the guns and mortars on their carriages and beds, had to be done almost exclusively at night, alike regardless of the inclemency of the weather, and of the miasma from the swamps.

61. No one except an eye-witness, can form any but a faint conception of the Herculean labor by which mortars of eight and one half tons weight, and columbiads but a trifle lighter, were moved in the dead of night, over a narrow causeway, bordered by swamps on either side, and liable at any moment to be overturned, and buried in the mud beyond reach. The stratum of mud is about twelve feet deep; and on several occasions the heaviest pieces, particularly the mortars, became de-

tached from the sling-carts, and were with great difficulty, by the use of planks and skids, kept from sinking to the bottom. Two hundred and fifty men were barely sufficient to move a single piece, on sling-carts. The men were not allowed to speak above a whisper, and were guided by the notes of a whistle.

62. The positions selected for the five most advanced batteries, were artificially screened from view from the fort, by a gradual and almost imperceptible change, made little by little every night, in the condition and appearance of the brushwood and bushes in front of them. No sudden alteration of the outline of the landscape was permitted. After the concealment was once perfected to such a degree as to afford a good and safe parapet behind it, less care was taken; and some of the work in the batteries requiring mechanical skill, was done in the daytime, the fatigue parties going to their labor before break of day, and returning in the evening, after dark.

63. In all the batteries, traverses were placed between the pieces.

64. With two exceptions (batteries Lincoln and Totten), the magazines were placed in or near the centre of the battery, against the epaulement, with the opening to the rear. An ante-room for filling cartridge-bags was attached to each. The magazines for the batteries Lincoln and Totten were located in the rear of the platforms.

65. For revetting the sides of traverses and epaulements, fascines, hurdles, brush, and marsh sods were used. Marsh sods form the best revetment for sandy soil. All the others allow the sand to sift through them to such an extent, as to become a serious annoyance to the men serving the pieces.

66. In order to diminish, as much as possible, the labor of forming the parapets in front of the pieces, the foundation timbers of all the gun and mortar platforms were sunk to high-water mark. This brought them, in many cases, to within six or eight inches of the substratum of soft clay. To secure them against settlement, the lateral as well as vertical dimensions usually adopted for platforms, were considerably enlarged.

67. Drawings of the mortar platforms, with bills of timber attached, are shown in Plate IV.

68. On the 31st day of March, Major-General Hunter assumed command of the Department of the South, and Brigadier-General Benham, of the northern district thereof, comprising the states of South Carolina, Georgia, and a part of Florida. During the week which followed, these generals visited Tybee Island at separate times, and inspected the siege works and batteries then established. No change or modification of any of the works was suggested by either.

69. On the afternoon of April 9th, every thing was in readiness to open fire. Generals Hunter and Benham had arrived the evening before, with their respective staffs.

70. The following general orders, regulating the rapidity and direction of the firing, and the charges and elevation of the pieces of each battery, were issued. As the instructions then given were, with one or two exceptions, adhered to with remarkable fidelity throughout the action, they are inserted here in full, to save the necessity of further reference to them.

71. HEADQUARTERS U. S. FORCES, TYBEE ISLAND, GA., *April 9th*, 1862.

General Orders. *No.* 17.

The batteries established against Fort Pulaski, will be manned and ready for service at break of day, to-morrow.

The signal to begin the action, will be one gun from the right mortar of battery Halleck (2,400 yards from the work), fired under the direction of Lieutenant Horace Porter, chief of ordnance. Charge of mortar, eleven pounds; charge of shell, eleven pounds; elevation, fifty-five degrees; length of fuze, twenty-four seconds.

This battery (two thirteen-inch mortars) will continue firing at the rate of fifteen minutes to each mortar, alternately, varying the charge of mortars and the length of fuze, so that the shells will drop over the arches of the north and north-east faces of the work, and explode immediately after striking, and not before.

The other batteries will open as follows, viz.:

Battery Stanton (three thirteen-inch mortars, 3,400 yards distant), immediately after the signal, at the rate of fifteen minutes for each piece, alternating from the right. Charge of mortars, fourteen pounds; charge of shell, seven pounds; elevation, forty-five degrees; and length of fuze, twenty-three seconds; varying the charge of mortar and length of fuze as may be required. The shells should drop over the arches of the south face of the work, and explode immediately after striking, but not before.

Battery Grant (three thirteen-inch mortars, 3,200 yards distant), immediately after the ranges of battery Stanton have been determined, at the rate of fifteen minutes for each piece, alternating from the right. Charge of shells, seven pounds; elevation, forty-five degrees; charges of mortars and length of fuze to be varied to suit the range, as determined from battery Stanton. The shells should drop over the south face of the work, and explode immediately after striking, but not before.

Battery Lyon (three ten-inch columbiads, 3,100 yards distant), with a curved fire, immediately after the signal, allowing ten minutes between the discharges for each piece, alternating from the right. Charge of gun, seventeen pounds; charge of shell, three pounds; elevation, twenty degrees; and length of fuze, twenty seconds; charge and length of fuze to vary as required. The shells should pass over the parapet into the work, taking the gorge and north face in reverse, and exploding at the moment of striking, or immediately after.

Battery Lincoln (three eight-inch columbiads, 3,045 yards distant), with a curved fire, immediately after the signal, allowing six minutes between discharges for each piece, alternating from the right. Charge of gun, ten pounds; charge of shell, one and one-half pounds; elevation, twenty degrees; and length of fuze, twenty seconds; directed the same as battery Lyon, upon the gorge and north face in reverse, varying the charge and length of fuze accordingly.

Battery Burnside (one thirteen-inch mortar, 2,750 yards distant) firing every ten minutes from the time the range is obtained for battery Sherman. Charge of shell, seven pounds; elevation, forty-five degrees; charge of mortar and length of fuze varying as required, from those obtained for battery Sherman. The shells should drop on the arches of the north and north-east faces, and explode immediately after striking, but not before.

Battery Sherman (three thirteen-inch mortars, 2,650 yards distant), commencing immediately after the ranges for battery Grant have been determined, and firing at the rate of fifteen minutes for each piece, alternating from the right. Charge of shell, seven pounds; elevation, forty-five degrees; charge of mortar and length of fuze to be fixed to suit the range, as determined from battery Grant. The shells should drop over the arches of the north and north-east faces.

Battery Scott (three ten-inch and one eight-inch columbiad, 1,740 yards distant), firing solid shot, and commencing immediately after the barbette fire of the work has ceased. Charge of ten-inch columbiads, twenty pounds; elevation, four and one-half degrees. Charge of eight-inch columbiad, ten pounds; elevation, five degrees.

This battery should breach the *pancoupé* between the south and south-east faces, and the embrasure next to it, in the south-east face; the elevation to be varied accordingly,—the charge to remain the same.

Until the elevation is accurately determined, each

gun should fire once in ten minutes; after that, every six or eight minutes.

Battery Sigel (five thirty-pounder Parotts, and one forty-eight-pounder James—old twenty-four pounder rifled—1,670 yards distant) to open with four and three-quarter seconds fuzes, on the barbette guns of the fort, at the second discharge from battery Sherman. Charge for thirty-pounder, three and one-half pounds; charge for forty-five-pounder, five pounds; elevation, four degrees for both calibres. As soon as the barbette fire of the work has been silenced, this battery will be directed with percussion shells upon the walls, to breach the pancoupé, between the south and south-east faces, and the embrasure next to it, in the south-east face; the elevation to be varied accordingly,—the charge to remain the same. Until the elevation is actually determined, each gun should fire once in six or eight minutes; after that, every four or five minutes.

Battery McClellan (two eighty-four and two sixty-four-pounders, James—old forty-two and thirty-two-pounders, rifled—1,650 yards distant) opens fire immediately after battery Scott. Charge for eighty-four-pounder, eight pounds; charge for sixty-four-pounder, six pounds; elevation for eighty-four-pounder, four and one-quarter degrees; and sixty-four-pounder, four degrees. Each piece should fire once every five or six minutes, after the elevation has been established; charge to remain the same.

This battery should breach the work in the pan coupé, between the south and south-east faces, and the embrasure next to it, in the south-east face.

The steel scraper, for the grooves, should be used after every fifth or sixth discharge.

Battery Totten (four ten-inch siege mortars, 1,650 yards distant) opens fire immediately after battery Sigel, firing each piece about once in five minutes. Charge of mortar, three and one-half pounds; charge of shell, three pounds; elevation, forty-five degrees; and length of fuze, eighteen and one-half seconds. The charge of mortar and length of fuze to vary, so as to explode the shells over the north-east and south-east faces of the work.

If any battery should be unmasked outside the work, battery Totten will direct its fire upon it, varying the charge and length of fuze accordingly.

The fire from each battery will cease at dark, except especial directions be given to the contrary.

A signal officer at battery Scott, to observe the effects of the thirteen-inch shells, will be in communication with other signal officers stationed near batteries Stanton, Grant, and Sherman, in order to determine the ranges for these batteries in succession.

By order of

Brig. Gen. Q. A. GILLMORE.

W. L. M. BURGER,

1st. Lieut. Vol. Eng. & Act'g. Asst. Adj. Gen.

72. Just after sunrise, on the morning of the 10th, Major-General David Hunter, commanding the department, dispatched Lieutenant J. H. Wilson, of the Topographical Engineers, to Fort Pulaski, bearing a flag of truce, and a summons to surrender.

To this demand a negative answer was returned.

73. The order was given to open fire, commencing

with the mortar batteries, agreeably to the foregoing instructions.

74. The first shell was fired at a quarter past eight o'clock, A. M., from battery Halleck. The other mortar batteries opened one after the other, as rapidly in succession as it was found practicable to determine the approximate ranges, by the use of signals. The guns and columbiads soon followed, so that before half-past nine, A. M., all the batteries were in operation; it having been deemed expedient not to wait for the barbette fire of the work to be silenced, before opening with breaching-batteries Scott and McClellan.

75. The three ten-inch columbiads in battery Scott were dismounted by their own recoil, at the first discharge; and one of those in battery Lyon, from the same cause, at the third discharge (see report of the ordnance officer, paragraph twenty-nine). They were all, except one in battery Scott, subsequently remounted and served.

76. As the several batteries along our line, which was 2,550 yards in length, opened fire one after another, the enemy followed them up successively, with a vigorous, though not at first very accurate fire, from his barbette and casemate guns. Subsequent inquiry showed that he knew the exact position of only two of our batteries (Sherman and Burnside). These were established just above high-water mark, on low ground, void of bushes or undergrowth of any kind. During their construction, no special attempt at concealment

had been made, after once securing good parapet cover by night-work.

77. Great disappointment was expressed, by all experienced officers present, at the unsatisfactory results obtained with the thirteen-inch mortars. Although the platforms were excellent, and remained, for all useful purposes, intact,—and although the pieces were served with a very fair degree of care and skill, not one-tenth of the shells thrown appeared to fall within the work; an estimate that was afterwards found to be rather over than under the correct proportion. Whether this inaccuracy is due to the fact that no cartridge-bags were furnished for the mortars, to inequalities in the strength of the powder, to defects inherent in the piece itself, or to these several causes combined, remains yet to be ascertained. It is suggested that the earnest attention of the proper department be directed to this subject.

78. By one o'clock in the afternoon (April 10th), it became evident that the work would be breached, provided our breaching batteries did not become seriously disabled by the enemy's fire. By the aid of a powerful telescope, it could be observed that the rifled projectiles were doing excellent service; that their penetration was deep and effective; and that the portion of the wall where the breach had been ordered, was becoming rapidly "honey-combed."

79. It also became evident before night, on account of the inefficiency of the mortar firing, that upon breach-

Plate VI. Oblique view of breach. Taken from the crest of counter-scarp, at high tide.
(6½ feet water in the ditch. Breach entirely practicable at low water.)

Plate VII. Front view of breach, taken from the opposite side of ditch.

ing alone,—ending, perhaps, in an assault,—we must depend for the reduction of the work.

80. In order to increase the security of our advanced batteries, a tolerably brisk fire against the barbette guns of the fort, was kept up throughout the day. Probably from fifteen to twenty per cent. of the metal thrown from the breaching batteries, on the 10th, was expended in this way.

81. As evening closed in, rendering objects indistinct, all the pieces ceased firing, with the exception of two thirteen-inch mortars, one ten-inch mortar, and one thirty-pounder Parrott, which were served throughout the night, at intervals of fifteen or twenty minutes for each piece.

82. I extract as follows, from my preliminary report to Brigadier-General Benham, dated April 12th, 1862:

83. "The only plainly perceptible result of this cannonade of ten and a half hours' duration (on the 10th), the breaching batteries having been served but nine and a half hours, was the commencement of a breach in the easterly half of the pancoupé, connecting the south and south-east faces, and in that portion of the south-east face spanned by the two casemates adjacent to the pancoupé."

84. "The breach had been ordered in this portion of the scarp, so as to take in reverse, through the opening

formed, the powder magazine, located in the angle formed by the gorge and the north face."

85. "Two of the barbette guns of the fort had been disabled, and three casemate guns silenced."

"The enemy served both tiers of guns briskly throughout the day, but without injury to the *matériel* or *personnel* of our batteries."

* * * * * *

86. "On the morning of the 11th, a little after sunrise, our batteries again opened fire with decided effect, the fort returning a heavy and well-directed fire from its casemate and barbette guns. The breach was rapidly enlarged. After the expiration of three hours, the entire casemate next the pancoupé had been opened, and by twelve o'clock, the one adjacent to it was in a similar condition."

87. "Directions were then given to train the guns upon the third embrasure, upon which the breaching batteries were operating with effect, when the fort hoisted the white flag. This occurred at two o'clock."

88. "The formalities of visiting the fort, receiving its surrender, and occupying it with our troops, consumed the balance of the afternoon and evening."

89. During the 11th, about one-tenth of the projectiles from the three breaching batteries, were directed against the barbette guns of the fort. Eleven of its guns were dismounted, or otherwise rendered temporarily unserviceable.

90. The garrison of the fort was found to consist of 385 men, including a full complement of officers. Several of them were severely, and one fatally wounded.

91. Our total loss was one man killed. None of our pieces were struck.

92. I take pleasure in recording my acknowledgment of the hearty, zealous and persevering co-operation afforded me by the officers and men under my command, not only during the 10th and 11th, when all more or less forgot their fatigue, in the excitement and danger of the engagement, but throughout the exhausting and unwholesome labors of preparation, occupying day and night, a period of nearly eight weeks.

93. The entire available strength of the command was on guard or fatigue duty every twenty-four hours.

94. The details for night-work were always paraded immediately after sunset, and were usually dismissed from labor between one and two o'clock in the morning, although circumstances frequently required parties to remain out all night.

95. In unloading the ordnance and ordnance stores, advantage was always taken of favorable tide and weather, day and night.

96. There is one circumstance connected with this siege, which appears to deserve special mention, and that is, that with the exception of a detachment of

sailors from the frigate Wabash, who served four of the light siege-pieces in battery Sigel, on the 11th, we had no artillerists of any experience whatever. Four of the batteries were manned by the Rhode Island volunteer artillery, who were conversant with the manual of the pieces, but had never been practised at firing. All the other pieces were served by infantry troops, who had been on constant fatigue duty, and who received all their instruction in gunnery at such odd times as they could be spared from other duties, during the week or ten days preceding the action.*

97. Throughout the siege, Colonel Alfred H. Terry, seventh regiment Connecticut volunteers, and Lieutenant Colonel James F. Hall, commanding battalion of New York volunteer engineers, were conspicuous for the zeal and perseverance with which they discharged the varied duties to which they were assigned.

98. Captain Hinkle, with one company of the forty-sixth regiment New York volunteers, and a small battery, occupied for eight weeks, with credit to himself and command, an advanced and exposed position on a hulk in Lazaretto Creek, cutting off boat communication in that direction, between Fort Pulaski and the interior.

* Instructions had been given by General Benham to place a mortar battery on the lower end of Long Island, and two ten-inch columbiads on Turtle Island, in order to obtain a reverse fire on the work. These batteries were to have been erected and manned by detachments from General Viele's command.

One ten-inch siege mortar was therefore placed on Long Island, and was served on the 11th April, by a detachment commanded by Major Beard, 48th New York volunteers. It was entirely ineffective on account of the distance, nearly 1,900 yards.

The idea of the Turtle Island battery was not carried into effect, and no pieces were landed there.

99. Lieutenant Horace Porter, of the ordnance department, rendered important and valuable service. Besides discharging, most efficiently, the special duties of chief of ordnance and artillery, he directed in person the transportation of nearly all the heavy ordnance, and instructed the men in its use. He was actively engaged among the batteries during the action.

100. Captain Charles E. Fuller, assistant quartermaster, served with me four weeks, assuming during that time the entire charge of unloading the ordnance and ordnance stores from the vessels, a duty which he discharged with a success worthy of special notice.

101. Lieutenant James H. Wilson, topographical engineers, joined my command eleven days before the action, and was assigned to duty as instructor of artillery. He rendered valuable service in that capacity, and also at the breaching batteries, on the 10th and 11th.

102. Captain Louis H. Pelouze, fifteenth United States infantry, and Captain J. W. Turner, commissary of subsistence, United States army, members of Major-General Hunter's staff, volunteered for the engagement, and were assigned to the command of batteries, where their knowledge and experience as artillerists proved of great value.

103. On the 11th, two pieces of battery Sigel were served by a detachment from the eighth regiment Maine volunteers, under Captain McArther, of that regiment.

The men had all served exclusively as infantry, and received their first artillery drill from Captain Turner and Lieutenant Wilson, under a severe fire. They readily adapted themselves to their new duties, .and served their guns creditably.

104. Captain F. E. Graef and Lieutenant T. B. Brooks, commanding respectively the two companies (D and A) of volunteer engineers, were indefatigable in the discharge of their duties as engineer officers, which required them to be out with the working parties every night.

105. I am under obligations to Commander C. R. P. Rodgers and Lieutenant John Irwin, United States navy, for skilfully serving, with a detachment of sailors, four siege-guns in battery Sigel, on the 11th.

106. Lieutenant W. L. M. Burger, of the regiment of New York volunteer engineers, served with zeal and efficiency as my adjutant-general, during the operations on Tybee Island.

107. Lieutenant P. H. O'Rorke, of the corps of engineers, and Adam Badeau, Esq., volunteered to serve as my aids on the 10th and 11th, and rendered valuable assistance.

108. The services of Sergeant James E. Wilson, of Company A, corps of engineers, deserve special mention, and largely contributed toward getting the breaching batteries ready for service.

Sergeant Wilson commanded battery Burnside during the action.

109. To Major-General Hunter, and Brigadier-General Benham, commanding respectively this department and district, I am under obligations for the official courtesy with which they allowed the project for reducing the fort, which was planned and all but executed before they assumed their commands, to be carried out in all its details, without change or modification.

GENERAL OBSERVATIONS.

110. The three breaching batteries, Sigel, Scott and McClellan (see Plates II. and III.), were established at a mean distance of 1,700 yards from the scarp walls of Fort Pulaski.

111. The circumstance, altogether new in the annals of sieges, that a practicable breach was made at that distance, in a wall 7½ feet thick, standing obliquely to the line of fire, and backed by heavy casemate piers and arches, cannot be ignored by a simple reference to the time-honored military maxims that "*Forts cannot sustain a vigorous land attack*," and that "*all masonry should be covered from land batteries.*"

112. A comparative glance at the status of military science, as regards breaching, prior to the invention of rifled cannon, will enable us to form a tolerably correct estimate of the importance to be attached to the results developed by this improved arm of the service

113. A standard military work furnishes the following extract:

"An exposed wall may be breached with certainty at distances from 500 to 700 yards, even when elevated 100 feet above the breaching battery; and it is believed that in case of extreme necessity, it would be justifiable to attempt to batter down an exposed wall from any distance not exceeding 1,000 yards, but then the quantity of artillery must be considerable, and it will require from four to seven days' firing, according to the number of guns in battery and the period of daylight, to render a breach practicable."

114. During the Peninsular War, breaching at 500 to 700 yards was of frequent occurrence, and at the second siege of Badajos, fourteen brass twenty-four-pounders breached an exposed castle wall backed by earth alone (and consequently much weaker than a scarp sustained in the rear by heavy piers and arches), in eight hours, at a distance of 800 yards.

115. Experiments at breaching with rifled guns have recently been made. I shall notice two cases:

116. In August, 1860, experiments with Armstrong's rifled guns were made against a condemned Martello Tower, at Eastbourne, on the coast of Sussex, England. The tower was of brick, fifty-six years old, and designed for one gun, the wall being seven and a half feet thick at the level of the ground, and five and three-fourths feet thick at the spring of the vault, which was

nineteen feet above the ground. It was thirty-one and a half feet high, forty-six feet exterior diameter at the bottom, and forty feet at the top.

117. The pieces used against it were, one forty-pounder of four and three-fourths inches calibre, one eighty-two-pounder of six inches calibre, and one seven-inch howitzer throwing 100 lb. shells.

118. A practicable breach twenty-four feet wide, including most of the arch, was made with an expenditure of 10,850 pounds of metal, at the distance of 1,032 yards.

119. The projectiles expended were:

40-pounder gun,	20 solid shot,	1 plugged shell,	43 live shells.
82 " "	19 " "	8 " "	36 " "
7-inch howitzer,		2 " "	29 " "

Projectiles that failed to hit the wall are excluded from the above table.

120. General Sir John Burgoyne in his report upon these experiments, says: "*Trials were subsequently made to breach a similar tower from smooth-bored sixty-eight and thirty-two-pounders, at the same range of* 1,032 *yards, and the result may be deemed altogether a failure, both accuracy of fire and velocity of missiles being quite deficient for such a range.*"

"*At* 500 *or perhaps* 600 *yards, the superiority of the rifled ordnance would probably have been very little, if any.*"

121. Experimental siege operations for the instruc-

tion of the Prussian army, comprising the demolition of the defective and obsolete fortifications at Juliers, were carried on in the month of September, 1860, especially with reference to the effect of rifled breech-loading guns.

122. The following brief summary of the breaching experiments, is taken from the report of Lieut.-Col. A. Ross, Royal Engineers :

123. "Four twelve-pounder iron guns, and two twelve-pounder brass guns, weighing respectively 2,700 pounds and 1,300 pounds, throwing a conical ball weighing twenty-seven pounds, and fired with a charge of two and one-tenth pounds, at 800 Prussian paces (640 yards), made a practicable breach thirty-two feet wide in a brick wall three feet thick, with counterforts four feet thick, four feet wide, and sixteen feet from centre to centre, the wall being sixteen feet high and built *en décharge*, after firing 126 rounds. The first six rounds are omitted from this calculation, as they did not strike the wall, the wall being entirely covered from the guns."

"No difference was observed between the effects of the brass and the iron guns. The bursting-charge of the shells was fourteen-fifteenths of a pound. The penetration was fifteen inches."

124. "Six six-pounder guns, four of iron and two of cast steel, weighing respectively 1,300 and 800 pounds, throwing a conical shell weighing thirteen pounds, and firing with a charge of one and one-tenth pounds, at

fifty paces, made a practicable breach seventy feet wide, in precisely the same description of wall as that above described, after firing 276 rounds, the battery being situated on the counterscarp opposite the wall."

"No difference was observed between the effects of the cast-steel and iron guns."

"The bursting-charge of a shell was half a pound. The penetration of the first single shots averaged eighteen inches."

125. "Four 24-pdr. iron guns, weighing between 53 and 54 cwt., throwing a shell weighing fifty-seven pounds, and fired with a charge of four pounds, at a distance of sixty yards, made a practicable breach sixty-two feet wide, in a loop-holed brick wall twenty-four feet high and six and a half feet thick, after firing 117 rounds, the wall being seen from the battery. The bursting-charge of the shell was two pounds. The penetration of the two first single shots was two and a half and three feet."

126. "The same guns, after firing 294 rounds with the same charges, and at a distance of ninety-six yards, made a breach forty-six feet wide in a brick wall forty feet high and twelve feet thick at the foot, with a batter of about four feet. The wall was twelve feet thick, and built *en décharge*, with counterforts six feet wide and sixteen feet from centre to centre, and connected by two rows of arches one above the other. The penetration of the first single shots was three feet and three and a half feet. All the above-mentioned guns were rifled breech-loaders."

127. It is impossible to institute a very close comparison of the relative value of rifled and smooth-bored guns for breaching purposes, from any data which experience has thus far developed.

128. The experiments at Eastbourne, hereinbefore mentioned, are the only ones on record, where they have been tried side by side, to the extent of actual breaching, against the same kind of masonry, and at the same distance.

We have seen how on that occasion the rifles were a complete success, while the smooth-bores were an utter failure.

129. At Fort Pulaski an excellent opportunity was afforded on the scarp wall near the breach, for obtaining the actual penetration of the several kinds of projectiles. An average of three or more shots for each calibre was taken, giving the following results, which may be relied upon as correct:

Table of penetrations in a brick wall, as determined at the siege of Fort Pulaski, Georgia, April, 1862.

Kind of Gun.	Distance from Wall.	Kind and weight of projectile.	Elevation.	Charge.	Penetration.
Old 42-pdr. rifled,	1650 yards,	James' 84 lb. solid,	$4\frac{1}{4}$ deg.	8 lbs.	26 in's.
" 32 " "	1650 "	" 64 " "	4 "	6 "	20 "
" 24 " "	1670 "	" 48 " "	$4\frac{1}{2}$ "	5 "	19 "
Parrott rifled guns,	1670 "	Parrott 30 " "	$4\frac{1}{2}$ "	$3\frac{1}{2}$ "	18 "
10-in. Columbiad, smooth bore,	1740 "	128 lb. solid, round,	$4\frac{1}{2}$ "	20 "	13 "
8-in. Columbiad, smooth bore,	1740 "	68 " " "	5 "	10 "	11 "

130. The above table indicates very prominently, al though it affords no exact means of measuring, the great

superiority of rifled over smooth-bored guns, for purposes requiring great penetrating power.

131. Against brick walls the breaching effect of percussion shells is certainly as great as that of solid shot of the same calibre. They do not penetrate as far by twenty to twenty-five per cent., but by bursting they make a much broader crater. Such shells would doubtless break against granite walls, without inflicting much injury.

132. Sir W. Dennison, from a comparison of the several sieges in Spain during the Peninsular War, estimated that a practicable breach at 500 yards could be made in a rubble wall, backed by earth, by an average expenditure of 254,400 lbs. of metal, fired from smooth-bore 24-pdrs. for every 100 feet in width of breach: equal to 2,544 lbs. of metal for every lineal foot in width of breach.

133. Before we can draw any comparison, however imperfect, between this estimate and the results obtained at Fort Pulaski, it is necessary to make certain deductions from the amount of metal thrown from the breaching batteries used against that work, as follows:

First. For the shots expended upon the barbette guns of the fort in silencing their fire.

Second. For ten per cent. of Parrott's projectiles which upset, from some defect which, I know from personal observation, has been entirely removed by the recent improvements of the manufacturer.

Third. For nearly fifty per cent. of the 64-lb. James

shot, due to the fact that one of the two pieces from which they were thrown had, by some unaccountable oversight, been bored nearly one-fourth of an inch too large in diameter, and gave no good firing whatever. Making these deductions, it results that 110,643 lbs. of metal were fired at the breach.

The really practicable portion of the breach was of course only the two casemates that were fully opened, say thirty feet in aggregate width, but the scarp wall was battered down in front of three casemate piers besides; and had these piers not been there, or had the scarp been backed by earth alone, as was generally the case in Spain, the practicable portion of the opening would have been from forty-five to fifty feet wide. Calling it forty-five feet, the weight of metal thrown per lineal foot of breach was 2,458 lbs., against 2,544 per lineal foot in the Peninsular sieges. Had the fort held out a few hours longer this difference would have been much greater, for the wall was so badly shattered to the distance of twenty-five or thirty feet each side of the breach, that the opening could have been extended either way with a comparatively trifling expenditure of metal. On repairing the work one hundred lineal feet of the scarp wall had to be rebuilt.

134. It must be borne in mind that at Fort Pulaski only fifty-eight per cent. of the breaching metal was fired from rifled guns, the balance being from the smooth-bored 8-inch and 10-inch columbiads (68 and 128-pdrs.) of battery Scott.

135. It may therefore be briefly and safely announced

that *the breaching of Fort Pulaski at* 1,700 *yards, did not require as great an expenditure of metal, although but fifty-eight per cent. of it was thrown from rifled guns, as the breaches made in Spain with smooth-bores exclusively, at* 500 *yards.* In the former case the wall was good brick masonry, laid in lime mortar, and backed by heavy piers and arches; in the latter, rubble masonry backed by earth.

136. A knowledge of the relative value of heavy round shot, ten-inch for example, and elongated percussion shells from lighter guns, say James' 64-pounders (old thirty-two-pounders), in bringing down the masses of brick masonry cracked and loosened by the elongated solid shot, is a matter of some importance, considering the vast difference in the amount of labor required to transport and handle the two kinds of ordnance. The penetration of the percussion shell would exceed, and its local effect would at least equal, that of the solid round shot. The general effect of the latter, within certain ranges, is a matter for consideration.

137. My own opinion, based principally upon personal observation, corroborated by the reports of experiments made in Europe, may be stated in the following terms:

138. *First.* Within 700 yards, heavy smooth-bores may be advantageously used for breaching, either alone, or in combination with rifles.

139. *Second.* Within the same distance, light smooth-

bores will breach with certainty, but rifles of the same weight are much better.

140. *Third.* Beyond 700 yards, rifled guns exclusively are much superior for breaching purposes, to any combination of rifles and heavy or light smooth-bores.

141. *Fourth.* Beyond 1,000 yards, a due regard to economy in the expenditure of manual labor and ammunition, requires that smooth-bores, no matter how heavy they may be, should be scrupulously excluded from breaching batteries.

142. *Fifth.* In all cases when rifled guns are used exclusively against brick walls, at least one-half of them should fire percussion shells. Against stone walls, shell would be ineffective.

143. For breaching at long distances, the James and Parrott projectiles seem to be all that can be desired. The grooves of the James gun must be kept clean at the seat of the shot. This is not only indispensably necessary, but of easy and ready attainment, by using the very simple and effective scraper, devised on the principle of the searcher, for the pieces we employed against Pulaski. This scraper consists of a number of steel springs or prongs—one for each groove—firmly attached by screws to the cylindrical part of a rammer head, and flaring like a broom, so as to fit closely into the grooves. About half an inch of the lower end of each prong is bent out at right angles. The prongs, being compressed by a ring, to which a lan-

yard is attached when entering the bore, spring out firmly into the grooves, when the ring is removed, and cleans them thoroughly, as the scraper is drawn out.

The failure of the James shot as reported on two or three occasions, by apparently good authority, is probably due to neglect in this particular. There were no failures in our firing, except as before mentioned, with the thirty-two-pounder (carrying a sixty-four pound shot) that had been bored too large.

144. Although the James projectiles are surrounded when first made, by greased canvas, there is believed to be an advantage in greasing them again at the moment of loading. This was done in our batteries against Fort Pulaski. As the Parrott projectiles receive their rotary motion from a ring of wrought iron or brass which surrounds the lower portion of the cylinder, and which does not foul the grooves while engaging them, no special precautions to prevent "fouling" need be taken with the Parrott guns. *With heavy James or Parrott guns, the practicability of breaching the best-constructed brick scarp, at* 2,300 *to* 2,500 *yards with satisfactory rapidity, admits of very little doubt. Had we possessed our present knowledge of their power, previous to the bombardment of Fort Pulaski, the eight weeks of laborious preparation for its reduction, could have been curtailed to one week, as heavy mortars and columbiads would have been omitted from the armament of the batteries, as unsuitable for breaching at long ranges.**

* For a brief description of certain projectiles, see Appendix F.

145. *It is also true beyond question, that the minimum distance, say from* 900 *to* 1,000 *yards, at which land batteries have heretofore been considered practically harmless against exposed masonry, must be at least trebled, now that rifled guns have to be provided against.*

146. The inaccuracy of the fire of the thirteen-inch mortars has already been adverted to. Not one-tenth of the shells dropped inside of the fort. A few struck the terre-plein over the casemate arches, but so far as could be observed by subsequent inspection from below, without producing any effect upon the masonry. Whether they penetrated the earth-work to the roofing of the arches, was not ascertained.

147. Two or three, striking in rapid succession in the same spot, over an arch, might be expected to injure it seriously, if not fatally. Such an occurrence would, however, be rare indeed. Against all except very extraordinary casualties, it would be easy for a garrison to provide as they occurred, by repairing with sand-bags or loose earth, the holes formed in the *terre-plein* by shells.

148. We may therefore assume, that *mortars are unreliable for the reduction of a good casemated work of small area, like most of our sea-coast fortifications.*

149. As auxiliary in silencing a barbette fire, or in the reduction of a work containing wooden buildings, and other exposed combustible material, mortars may undoubtedly be made to play an important part.

150. For the reduction of fortified towns or cities, or extensive fortresses, containing large garrisons, there is perhaps no better arm than the mortar, unless it be the rifled gun firing at high elevations.

151. To the splinter-proof shelters, constructed for the seven advanced batteries, I attribute our almost entire exemption from loss of life. We had one man killed by a shell from one of the mortar batteries outside the fort, which was the only casualty.

152. A cross section of the splinter-proof shelters is shown on Plate III. The same plate shows the position of these shelters for the breaching batteries and battery Totten, and of the surgery, which was constructed in most respects like the splinter-proofs, with the exception of its being six and a half feet in height.

153. The demoralizing effect of constant and laborious fatigue duty, upon the health and discipline of troops, particularly upon such as are unused to the privations of war, like our volunteers, who can but slowly adapt themselves to the stinted comforts of a campaign, is a subject which demands the earnest attention of commanding officers in the field.

154. Upon regular troops, to whom the drill in their special arm has, to a certain extent, become a second nature, who are accustomed to the vicissitudes of the field, and familiar with expedients and "make-shifts" to secure comfort, the bad effects of excessive labor and

constant interruption of drill, are of course less apparent.

155. With the average of our volunteer regiments, every alternate day should be devoted to drill, in order to keep them up to a fair standard of efficiency.

Very respectfully, your obedient servant,

Q. A. GILLMORE,
Brig.-Gen. Vols.

To Brig.-Gen. J. G. TOTTEN,
Chief Eng. U. S. A., Wash., D. C.

APPENDIX A.

LETTER FROM CAPTAIN GILLMORE, CHIEF ENGINEER EXPEDITIONARY CORPS, TO BRIGADIER-GENERAL T. W. SHERMAN, COMMANDING EXPEDITIONARY CORPS.

EXTRACT.

HEADQUARTERS CHIEF ENGINEER'S OFFICE,
HILTON HEAD, S. C., *Dec.* 1*st*, 1861.

BRIGADIER-GENERAL T. W. SHERMAN,
Commanding E. C., Hilton Head, S. C.

SIR:—Agreeably to your orders, I proceeded in the steamer "Benj. Deford," on the afternoon of the 29th ult., to Tybee Island, to make a military reconnoissance of that locality.

* * * * * * *

The exact position of the battery controlling Wassaw Inlet,* has no bearing on the prominent points to which my attention was directed, namely: the propriety of occupying and holding the first Tybee Island, and the practicability (and, if deemed practicable, the best method) of reducing Fort Pulaski.

I deem the reduction of that work practicable by batteries of mortars and rifled guns, established on Tybee Island. I think it probable that a nearer position, on firm ground (although very shallow, and therefore ill adapted to mortars and sunken batteries), can be found on the island west of Tybee.

I would establish these batteries from twenty to twenty-five yards apart, one gun or one mortar in each, behind the ridge of sand on the shore, westward from the lighthouse.

I would sink the mortar batteries as low as the water would permit, and the guns sufficiently low to leave a high parapet in front. On the sides and rear of each, I would have a high mound of earth, and I would cover each with a horizontal bomb-proof shelter, of logs covered with earth, and supported by logs planted vertically in the ground.

The embrasures for the guns should be deep, narrow, and of very little splay. I estimate, that after once obtaining the range, five-eighths of the shells from the mortars can be lodged inside of the fort.

* The enemy had a battery on Wassaw Sound. Its exact position was not known at that time.

I would have enough mortars to throw one shell a minute into the fort, and as many guns as mortars.

For landing the ordnance required, I would have built two or three large flat-bottomed batteaus or scows, such as are commonly used on rope ferries. I think these could be built here.

There are now, probably, at Fort Pulaski, 700 good troops; about two hundred landed yesterday, and the navy officers informed me that at least five hundred have entered the fort within the last three days—while some (probably raw recruits, or portions of the home-guards) have gone away. It may be their design to land on Tybee, and hold the west end of it, to prevent the erection of batteries against the fort.

I therefore recommend the immediate occupation of Tybee Island by one good regiment, until the question of attempting the reduction of Fort Pulaski be determined.

I learned while at Tybee that offers have been made by negroes to burn two of the principal bridges on the railroad between Charleston and Savannah, one of these bridges is said to be nearly two miles long. In a military point of view, its destruction would be of great value to us, and I recommend the subject to your attention. Very respectfully,

Your obed't servant,

[Signed.] Q. A. Gillmore,
Captain and Chief Engineer Ex. Corps.

APPENDIX B.

LETTER FROM CAPTAIN GILLMORE TO GENERAL SHERMAN.

Office of Chief Engineer, E. C.,
Hilton Head, S. C., *Dec.* 5*th*, 1862.

Brigadier-General T. W. Sherman,
Commanding E. C., Hilton Head, S. C.

Sir:—Should it be determined to attempt the reduction of Fort Pulaski, from Tybee Island, I recommend the following armament for the batteries, inclusive of pieces held in reserve, to replace those dismounted, or otherwise rendered unserviceable:—

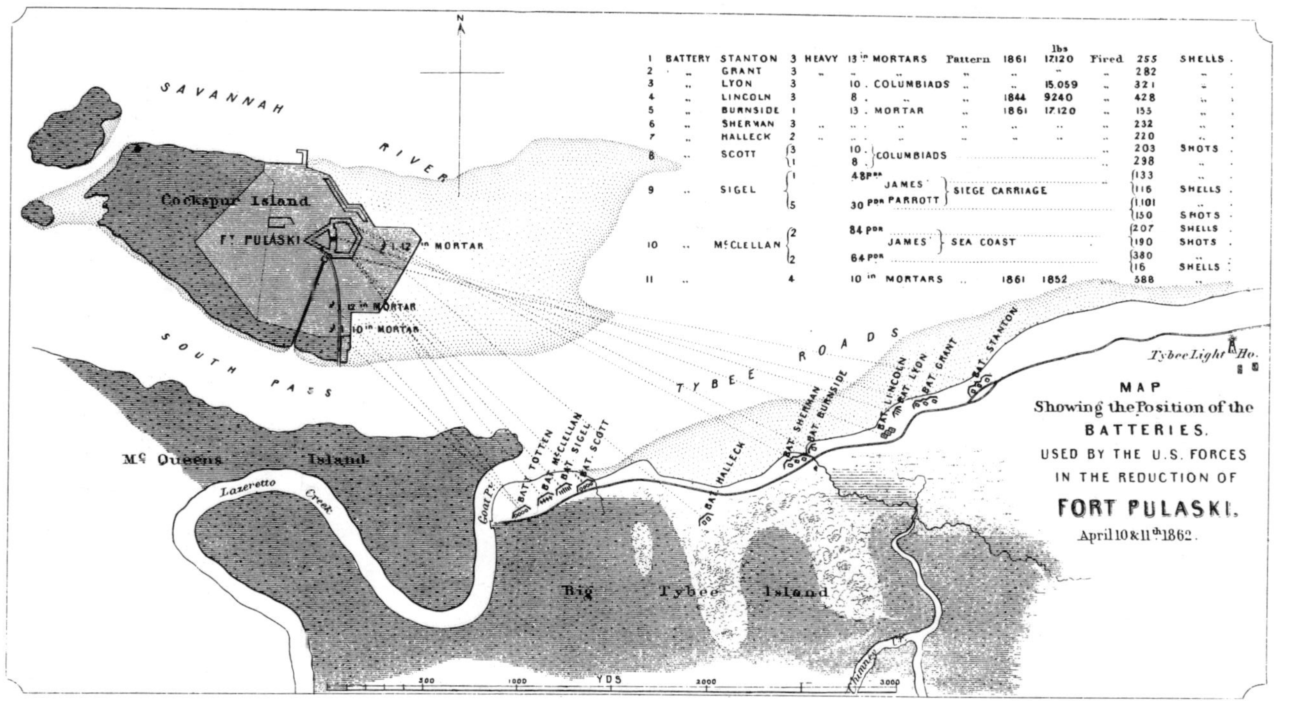

Plate II. Map: Batteries used by U.S. forces.

Plate I. Map: Mou

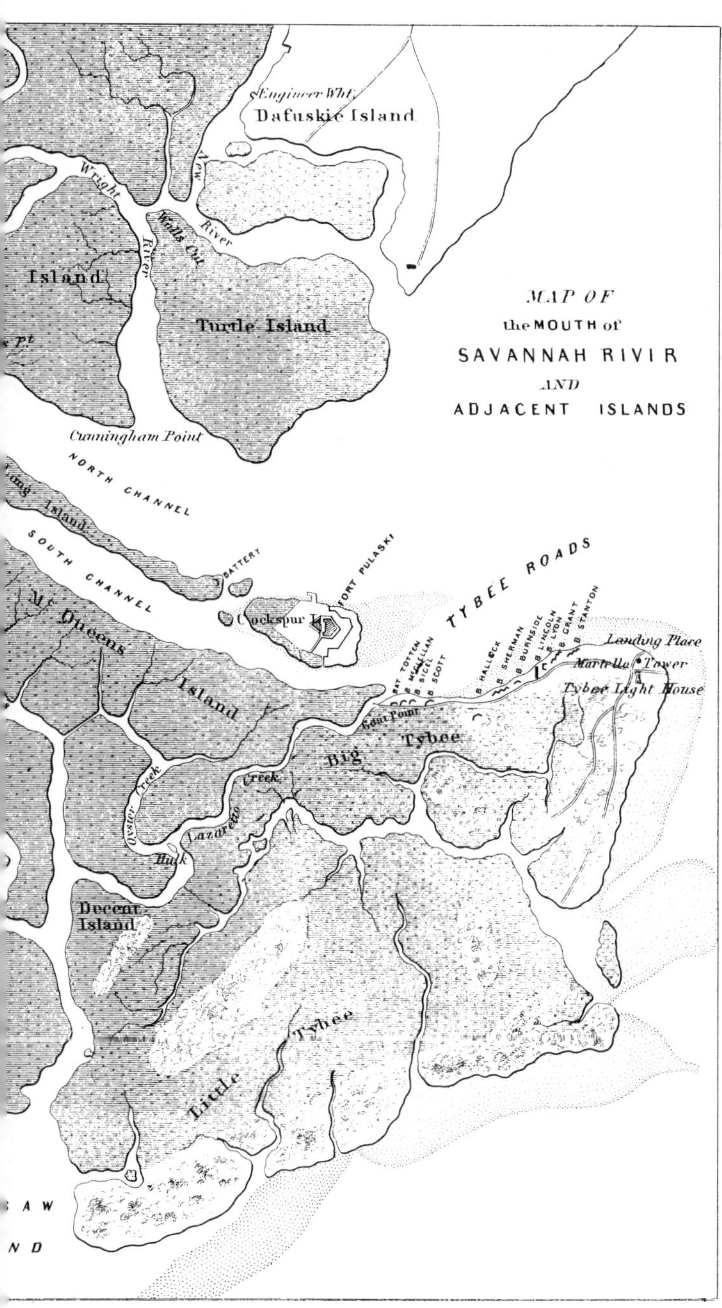

Savannah River.

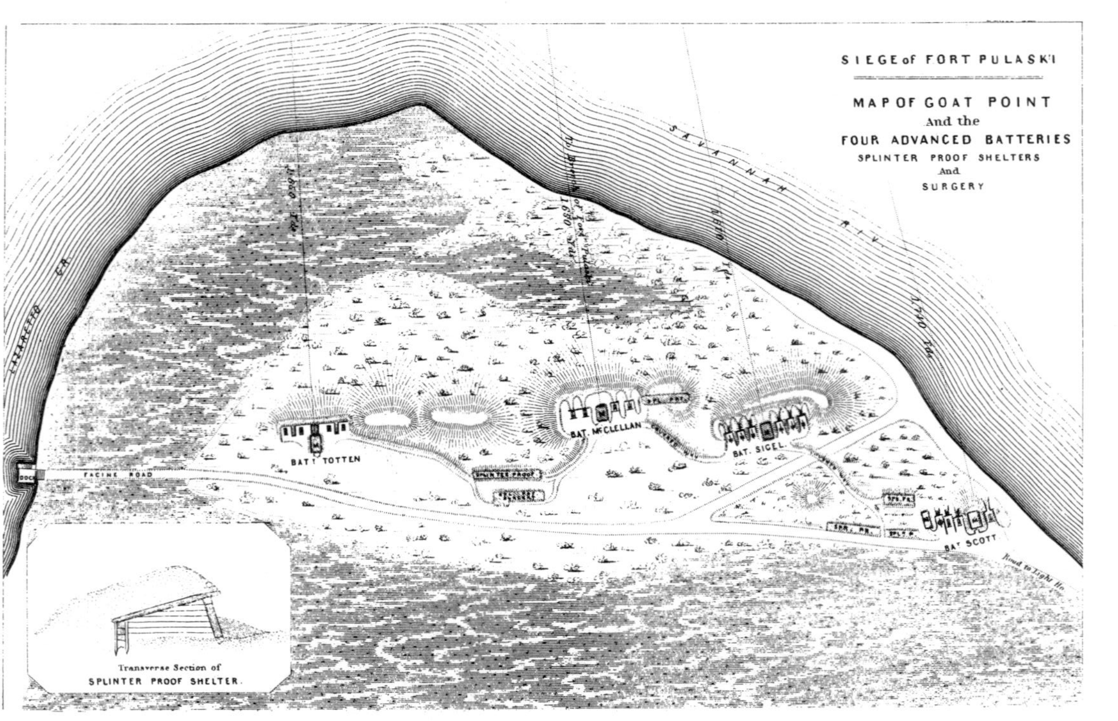

Plate III. Map: Goat Point.

Ten 10-inch sea-coast mortars.

Ten 13 " " "

Eight heavy rifled guns of the best kind, to be used, some against the barbette guns of the fort, and some against the walls.

Eight columbiads for firing solid shot, principally; some of them to fire shells, in case it be found practicable to drop them in, or explode them over the fort.

The mortars should each have 900 rounds of shells; the guns and columbiads the same number of rounds of solid shot, and the columbiads 300 rounds of shells beside.

It would be well to have a 15-inch columbiad, if one can be obtained. Very respectfully,

Your obed't servant,

[Signed.] Q. A. GILLMORE.

Captain and Chief Engineer E. C.

APPENDIX C.

HEADQUARTERS, TYBEE ISLAND, GA.,
April 8th, 1862.

SPECIAL ORDERS.
No. 32.

The following assignments to batteries is hereby made, viz:

1. BATTERY TOTTEN.

Capt. D. C. Rodman, 7th Conn. Vols.
" S. H. Gray, " " "
2d Lieut. S. J. Corey, " " "

with a detachment of the 7th Conn. Vols., in three reliefs.

2. BATTERY McCLELLAN.

Capt. H. Rogers,

with Company "H," 3d R. I. Vols., Artillery, in three reliefs.

3. BATTERY SIGEL.

Capt. S. Seldeneck, 46th N. Y. S. Vols.
" T. Hohle, " " "

with Co's "K and H," 46th N. Y. S. Vols., in three reliefs.

4. BATTERY SCOTT.

Capt. Pardon Mason,
with Company "F," 3d R. I. Vols., Artillery, in three reliefs.

5. BATTERY HALLECK.

Capt. O. S. Sanford, 7th Conn. Vols.
" E. S. Hitchcock, " " "
2d Lieut. S. S. Atwill, " " "
with a detachment of 7th Conn. Vols., in three reliefs.

6. BATTERY SHERMAN.

Capt. D. G. Francis, 7th Conn. Vols.
" J. B. Dennis, " " "
2d Lieut. V. B. Chamberlain, " " "
with a detachment of the 7th Conn. Vols., in three reliefs.

7. BATTERY BURNSIDE.

Sergt. James E. Wilson, Co. A, U. S. Engineers.
" P. Maguire, " " " " "
" Wadlie,
with a detachment of 8th Maine Vols., in three reliefs.

8 and 9. BATTERIES LINCOLN AND LYON.

Capt. Louis H. Pelouze, 15th U. S. Infantry, and Acting Inspector General, Department of the South; with Capt. L. E. Tourtelotte's Co. (B), 3d R. I. Vols., Artillery, in two reliefs.

10. BATTERY GRANT.

Capt. Charles E. Palmer, 7th Conn. Vols.
" Jerome Tourtelotte, " " "
1st Lieut. Wm. E. Phillip, " " "
with a detachment of 7th Conn. Vols., in three reliefs.

11. BATTERY STANTON.

Captain B. F. Skinner, 7th Conn. Vols.
" Theodore Beacon, " " "
1st Lt. Theodore Burdick, " " "
with a detachment of 7th Conn. Vols., in three reliefs.

By order of BRIG.-GEN. Q. A. GILLMORE.

W. L. M. BURGER,
1st Lieut. Vol. Engineers, A. Ass't. Adj.-Gen.

APPENDIX D.

REPORT OF LIEUTENANT HORACE PORTER, ORDNANCE DEPARTMENT, TO BRIGADIER-GENERAL GILLMORE.

FORT PULASKI, GA., *April* 12*th*, 1862.

SIR:—In compliance with directions from General Gillmore, I have the honor to submit the following report concerning the ordnance and ordnance stores used in the investment and bombardment of Fort Pulaski:

1. In obedience to an order from General T. W. Sherman, detailing me as ordnance officer to an expedition intended for the blockade of the Savannah River, and the interception of all communication in that direction with Fort Pulaski, I left Port Royal, with the ordnance selected for that purpose, January 26th, 1862.

2. The following pieces were carried in flat boats towed by a steamer;

4 30-pounder Parrott rifles.
3 20 " " "
2 8-inch siege howitzers.
1 24-pounder field howitzer.

Each flat carried the implements, equipments and ten rounds of ammunition for each of its guns.

A schooner followed containing:

5 24-pounder field howitzers.
3 24 " James rifles (old 12-pounders).
1 8-inch siege mortar,
1 10 " " "

200 rounds of ammunition per gun for all the pieces.

3. The boats lay at anchor in New River until Feb. 10th, guarded day and night by two companies of the 3d Rhode Island Vol. Artillery, Captains Gould and Bailey, whose skill and energy alone saved the flats during the long time they were exposed to rough waters, winds and tides.

4. An order was then received to place six of the pieces in position on Venus Point, Jones Island, about four miles from our anchorage.

5. Four flats, containing three 30-pounder Parrott rifles, two 20-pounder Parrott rifles, and one 8-inch siege howitzer, were taken in tow by row-boats, about five o'clock P. M., moved

through Walls Cut and Mud River, and landed at the temporary wharf on Jones Island at eight o'clock P. M. One 30-pounder gun and one 8-inch howitzer were first landed, and moved forward upon the island by Lieut. J. H. Wilson, Topographical Engineer, who volunteered his services for the occasion, and to whose energy the success of the undertaking is in a great measure due. After the remaining guns and ammunition had been landed and the boats secured, I moved forward two 30-pounder guns and was followed by Major Beard of the 48th N. Y. Volunteers with two 20-pounder guns. This officer volunteered to assist in the transportation of the artillery, and rendered most valuable service. The last gun was landed at ten o'clock P. M. Each officer had a detail of thirty-five men of the 48th N. Y. Volunteers.

6. Owing to some mistake they had been on duty during the previous twenty-four hours, and were totally unfit to undertake the task.

7. The actual difficulties of the undertaking commenced with the movement of the pieces across the island, nearly a mile in width. This island is a low marsh entirely under water during spring tides. Long planks were laid down forming a run-way for the wheels. The pieces were moved over them by hand, the planks taken up in rear and laid down in front, and so on. The men sunk to their knees at every step, the planks soon became covered with slimy mud, and the wheels frequently slipped off, sinking to the hubs and causing great delay and physical labor in prying them out. The men were soon unable to retain a hold upon the planks to carry them. Ropes were then attached, and they were dragged through the mud. The men were soon completely exhausted, many lay down in the mud and water unable to rise. About two o'clock, an order came from General Gillmore to suspend operations for the night. The first two pieces had advanced about four hundred yards. The guns were screened with reeds and grass, and left until the next night. With a fresh detail of men under the same officers the guns were then placed in position.

8. Lieutenant Wilson arrived at the battery about three o'clock. All the guns were in the battery ready to open fire by eight o'clock on the morning of the 11th.

9. The worst portion of the island was crossed the second night. Several times the men sunk down from physical exhaustion, and it required both encouragement and threats to keep enough by the guns to move them.

10. The river being now commanded, two 24-pounder field howitzers and fifty rounds of ammunition per gun for all the pieces were taken to the battery in boats by way of Wright River and the Savannah.

11. The remaining ammunition was left on board the schooner in charge of an ordnance sergeant, with directions to issue supplies upon requisitions from the officer commanding the battery.

12. The other guns remained in flats in New River. One boat containing one 20-pounder gun was swamped in consequence of a leak and the violence of the tides, and sunk in twelve feet water. The gun was soon after recovered uninjured.

13. An order was received February 20th to place six guns in battery on Bird's Island, opposite Jones' Island, in the Savannah. Boats had been collected and loaded during the two previous days, and select crews chosen for the row-boats.

14. About five o'clock P. M., on the above day, flats were towed through Walls Cut and Mud River, with one 8-inch siege howitzer, one 30-pounder Parrott rifle, one 20-pounder Parrott rifle, and three 24-pounder James rifles, each flat carrying the implements, equipments, and thirty rounds of ammunition for each of its guns. The boats reached the mouth of Mud River about twelve o'clock, and after waiting an hour for a change of tide pulled out into the Savannah. Major Beard, who had again volunteered his services, acted with his accustomed energy. He and Captain John Hamilton, 3d U. S. Artillery, Chief of Artillery on General Sherman's staff, kept in advance in a small boat, and, by signals given from time to time, indicated to the line of flats the proper direction, and enabled them to reach the island at the proper point, which was attended with some difficulty during the night, and while exposed to a strong tide. Such perfect silence was preserved by the men that the enemy's gunboats in the river were not aware of the movement until daylight, when it was too late to attack us.

15. We arrived at the upper end of the island at about two

o'clock. The platforms and magazines were constructed by the engineers during the remainder of the night, and at daylight an 8-inch howitzer was in position. The rest of the pieces were placed in the battery during the day, and by three o'clock could have opened fire. A hundred yards of marsh had to be crossed by the same method as that used upon Jones' Island. The guns were placed in position by details of men from Captain Bailey's Company of Third Rhode Island Artillery, and the Volunteer Engineers, Lieutenant Dalrymple of that regiment, and Major Beard labored most faithfully in the discharge of this duty.

16. Fifty rounds of ammunition per gun were placed in the magazine, and the remainder left in the schooner, from which it could be readily supplied.

17. In firing for ranges upon different points of the channel, I found that the Parrott guns fired with their usual accuracy with the exception of one 30-pounder, from which half of the projectiles turned end over end. The 8-inch siege howitzers gave very good results at 1,300 yards. The fuzes were exceedingly uniform.

18. Being ordered to Port Royal to collect ordnance for Tybee Island, I returned to that post February 22d, and started for Tybee Island February 24th.

19. The following ordnance and ordnance stores were landed at different times, and placed in position in the batteries opposite Fort Pulaski:

12	13-inch mortars and beds.		
4	10-inch siege mortars and beds.		
6	10-inch columbiads and carriages.		
4	8-inch "	"	
2	84-pounder James rifles,	"	(old 42-pounders rifled.)
2	64 " " "	"	(" 32 " ")
1	48 " " "	"	(" 24 " ")
5	30 " Parrott "	"	

Implements and equipments, and nearly 900 rounds of ammunition for each piece.

3,000 barrels of powder.

20. The heavy guns were landed by lowering them from the vessels into lighters, having a strong decking built across their gunwales. They were towed ashore by row-boats at high tide,

often in a heavy surf, and careened by means of a rope from shore, manned by soldiers, until the piece rolled off. At low tide this was dragged above high-water mark.

21. For the purpose of transporting the 13-inch mortars, weighing 17,000 pounds, a pair of skids was constructed of timber, ten inches square, and twenty feet long, held together by three cross-pieces, notched on. One end of the skids was lashed close under the axle of a large sling-cart, with the other end resting on the ground. The mortar was rolled up by means of ropes until it reached the middle of the skids, and checked. Another large sling-cart was run over the other end of the skids, which was raised by the screw, forming a temporary four-wheeled wagon. Two hundred and fifty men were required to move it over the difficult roads by which the batteries were reached.

22. I can pay no greater tribute to the patriotism of the 7th Connecticut Volunteers, the troops generally furnished me for this duty, than to say, that when the sling-carts frequently sank to their hubs in the marshes, and had to be extricated by unloading the mortar, rolling it upon planks, until harder ground could be found, and then reloading it, they toiled night after night, often in a drenching rain, under the guns of the fort, speaking only in whispers, and directed entirely by the sound of a whistle, without uttering a murmur. When drilling the same men in the mortar batteries, they exhibited an intelligence equalled only by their former physical endurance.

23. The 3d Rhode Island, 46th New York, and 8th Maine Volunteers moved several of the guns under similar difficulties.

24. Sergeant Wilson, Company A, U. S. Engineers, rendered important service in mounting the guns.

25. The 13-inch mortars were mounted by means of the ordinary garrison gin, by increasing the number of blocks, giving four sheaves above and three below. It was found that when the truck-wheels of the iron beds for the 13-inch mortars were thrown into gear they sank into the deck planks of the platforms, and did not relieve the cheeks of sufficient weight to enable the pieces to be moved to and from battery. Two pieces of flat iron, five feet long, four inches wide, and half an inch thick, were, at the suggestion of General Gillmore, let into the platforms under the wheels, projecting an eighth of an inch

above the surface, the inner edges two inches outside of the rails. The wheels then worked to perfection.

26. Notwithstanding the precautions constantly given the cannoniers at drill, five eccentric axle-stops on the 13-inch mortar beds were broken, but replaced before the firing commenced. One 10-inch columbiad eccentric axle-stop was broken during the firing, but did not interrupt the serving of the piece.

27. No difficulty was experienced in the ignition of the 13-inch mortar fuzes, nor in the use of friction tubes in those pieces.

28. The 13-inch mortar cartridge bags not having arrived, the powder was poured into the piece loose, and adjusted in the chamber by the gunner. This method was attended by very little more inconvenience than is experienced in smaller mortars.

29. The pintles and pintle crosses sent here were for the wooden barbette carriages, and caused the difficulty we experienced with the 10-inch columbiad iron carriages, front pintle. [See accompanying report of firing.] A collar was made for the pintle in order to bring it to the size of the pintle-hole. The chassis was not afterward thrown off the pintle.

30. The bolts which gave way in the iron carriages were injured, and several of them broken, by throwing the chassis from a boat upon the hard beach in landing. As these carriages were the last portion of the armament that arrived, no time was afforded for replacing the bolts before the firing commenced. When new bolts were put in during the first night of the bombardment, they remained uninjured by the next day's firing.

31. The two 84-pounder and two 64-pounder James rifle guns were used entirely in breaching, and gave the most satisfactory results, with the exception of one 64-pounder, many of the projectiles from which turned end over end.

32. The penetration of the 84-pounder shot into the brick masonry of the fort at 1,650 yards was twenty-five inches, of the 64-pounder twenty inches, and the shattering effect produced laterally very destructive. An examination of the walls proved conclusively that the projectiles entered point foremost, and many solid shots were found buried in the masonry in this

position. The shells exploded after penetrating about eighteen inches, and played an important part in reducing the work.

33. The penetration of an 84-pounder shot in an earthen traverse in the fort was twelve feet.

34. One great secret of the success of these guns, I think, was the constant use of a scraper for the grooves, proposed by General Gillmore. It was made upon the principle of the "searcher," by taking a number of strips of steel equal to the number of grooves in the piece, and of the same width, half an inch of one end bent up at a right angle. These were nailed along the cylindrical portion of a rammer head, at equal distances apart, giving the bent ends a flare. An iron ring was slipped over this to compress it when entering the bore, and then removed to let the scraper press well into the grooves. The scraper was used generally after every five or six shots. When not used for a longer time the effect was perceptible in the firing, and its constant use was afterward insisted upon.

35. There was not time to finish a scraper for the 48-pounder, and many of its shots were lost no doubt in consequence.

36. In regard to the James guns, the admirable manner in which the rifled motion is imparted to the projectile, the large mass of metal thrown, and the shape of the shot, seem to leave little to be desired in a breaching gun.

37. The Parrott guns being of smaller calibre (30-pounders) did not do the same execution; many of the projectiles turned end over end, and some took a *wabbling* motion in their flight, still many shots were found buried in the masonry point foremost with a penetration of eighteen inches, but exhibiting very little shattering effect. I think with larger calibres and carefully prepared projectiles, giving that accuracy of fire which these guns have been known to give, they would be found excellent for breaching purposes.

38. The *drift* of the rifled guns was about nine feet in a range of 1,670 yards.

39. The 2,293 shots fired from rifled guns during the two days of the bombardment give additional proof that the rifle projectile departs from a tangent to the trajectory and remains nearly parallel to its first position. The generally accepted theory accounting for *drift* has received another confirmation.

40. The 8 and 10-inch columbiads throwing solid shot at 1,740 yards performed their part admirably in the demolition of the masonry. The penetration of the 10-inch shot was thirteen inches, that of the 8-inch eleven inches when striking upon the untouched surface of the wall, and the lateral effect a little greater than that of the 84-pounder rifles; but it was after the latter guns had perforated the wall that the columbiads performed their true office in crushing out the immense masses of masonry.

41. The penetration of the different projectiles was ascertained by accurate measurement and a mean of several shots taken.

42. During both days of the bombardment the wind, which blew from right to left, was extremely unfavorable for mortar firing. This in connection with the fact that the gunners had never before fired a piece, and had been drilled only ten days, accounts in some degree for the loss of so many shells from the mortars.

43. The nearest 13-inch mortar, firing at an elevation of forty-five degrees, was 2,650 yards, and the farthest 3,400 yards; too great a distance for a successful vertical fire against a small area like that of the fort.

44. The 10-inch siege mortars at 1,650 yards dropped more than half their shells outside of the fort.

45. Many of the paper fuzes we were obliged to use in the absence of others, had been captured from the Rebel forces at Hilton Head, and were very inferior.

46. We are deeply indebted to the officers of the navy for furnishing us with a quantity of paper fuses, and flannel for making cartridge bags.

47. So much were the preparations hurried for opening the bombardment, that we could not wait for many of the ordnance stores that had been ordered from the north. Powder measures were made out of copper, from the metallic cases in which the desiccated vegetables are received. Columbiad shells were strapped with strips of old tents, rough blocks being used for sabots. A large party was kept working day and night, during the bombardment, making 10-inch Columbiad cartridge bags, and wooden fuze plugs for 10-inch mortars, in which paper fuzes were used.

48. For a detailed report of the firing, I refer you to the accompanying record.

49. The failure of many of the friction tubes, was owing to the fact that most of the cannoniers were unaccustomed to their use.

50. The recoil of the mortars increased slightly with the number of shots fired. The average recoil is given in the table.

51. Musket powder was used for filling the rifle shells. All the powder used in the pieces, was No. 5. Most of it Smith & Rand's, some Hazard's. I find the former gives a little greater range, not, I think, on account of the superior quality of the powder, but because there are more small grains in a given quantity, and the combustion is consequently more rapid. The 13-inch shells hold only about eight pounds of this size of powder, when loosely poured in.

52. None of the pieces became so hot during the bombardment, as to render it necessary to stop the firing.

53. The 13-inch mortars were fired once in ten or fifteen minutes. One was fired three times in fifteen minutes, without any extraordinary exertion on the part of the cannoniers.

54. Upon taking an inventory of the captured ordnance and ordnance stores in Fort Pulaski, the following were found, viz.*

5 10-inch columbiads, unchambered, from Tredegar Foundry.
9 8-inch " " 2 irreparable.
3 42-pounder guns.
20 32 " "
2 24 " rifled cannon, Blakely. English.
1 24 " howitzer, iron. Flank defence.
2 12 " " brass.
2 12-inch mortars, iron.
3 10-inch sea-coast mortars.
1 6-pounder gun.

6 10-inch columbiad carriages and chassis, one irreparable, one unserviceable.

10 8-inch columbiad carriages (seven barbette, three casemates) three irreparable, one unserviceable.

3 42-pounder carriages and chassis, casemate.

* Many small articles are omitted from Lieutenant Porter's list.

20 32-pounder carriages and chassis, casemate, two irreparable, one unserviceable.

2 24-pounder ship carriages, one irreparable.

1 24 " howitzer carriage and chassis. Flank defence.

2 24 " " " field.

2 12-inch mortar beds.

3 10-inch sea-coast mortar beds, one irreparable.

PROJECTILES UNPREPARED.

424 42-pounder shot.
2,600 32 " "
200 8-inch "
520 10 " columbiad shells.
1,000 8 " " "
45 12 " mortar "
150 10 " " "
700 10 " sabots.
250 8 " "
88 6-pounder shot.
100 24 " howitzer canister.
70 24 " rifle shells.

PROJECTILES PREPARED.

100 32-pounder spherical case.
36 12 " howitzer spherical case.
60 10-inch strapped shells.
80 8 " " "
400 32-pounder shells.
30 12 " howitzer canister.
61 12 " " shells.
87 6 " canister.

POWDER, AMMUNITION, &c.

40,000 pounds cannon powder.
200 " rifle "
500 " meal "

* * * *

The pieces bearing upon our batteries on Tybee Island are as follows:

In Barbette.

5 8-inch Columbiads.
4 10 " "
1 24-pounder rifle, Blakely.
2 10-inch sea-coast mortars.

In Casemate.

1 8-inch Columbiad.
4 32-pounder guns.

In Batteries outside the Fort.

1 10-inch sea-coast mortar.
2 12 " " "
Total, twenty pieces.

Respectfully submitted,
HORACE PORTER,
1*st Lieut. of Ordnance, U. S. A.*

To W. L. M. BURGER,
1*st Lieut. Vol. Eng. A. A. Adj.-Gen.*

TABULAR STATEMENT

Of the firing of the several Batteries at the Siege of Fort Pulaski, Georgia, April 10th and 11th, 1862.

Battery Stanton.

Days on which the firing occurred.	Description of pieces and carriages in the battery. Number of shots fired from each piece each day, and during both days. 1	2	3	4	5	6	Kind of projectile.	Charge for piece in pounds.	Charge for shell in pounds.	Elevation.	Length of fuze in seconds.	Distance from fort in yards.	State of wind, which blew from right to left.	Recoil of carriages. Feet.	Recoil of carriages. Inches.	Kind of powder used.	Number of friction tubes that failed.	Commenced firing.	Ceased firing.	Number of shots fired from this battery.
	13-inch Mortar, 1861. Iron bed.	13-inch Mortar, 1861. Iron bed.	13-inch Mortar, 1861. Iron bed.													No. 5. Hazard's, and Smith and Rand's.				
First day,	52	51	51				shells	14½	7	45°	27	3400	slight		4		10	8.20 a.m.	7 p.m	154
Second day,	34	34	33				"	"	"	"	"		strong				1	6.15 "	2 "	101
Total,	86	85	84														11			255

REMARKS.—Two shells were found too large for the bore. When within six inches of the powder they could be neither withdrawn nor forced down. They were fired in this position without injury to the piece.

Plate VIII. Interior view of breach, showing the two casemates that were opened.

Plate IX. Interior view of a portion of the Gorge, the Sally-Port, blindage in front of casemates used as Officers' Quarters, and a part of the parade dug into trenches to receive shells.
(Taken from the terre-plein of Southeast face.)

Battery Grant.

Days on which the firing occurred.	Description of pieces and carriages in the battery. Number of shots fired from each piece each day, and during both days.						Kind of projectile.	Charge for piece in pounds.	Charge for shell in pounds.	Elevation.	Length of fuze in seconds.	Distance from fort in yards.	State of wind, which blew from right to left.	Recoil of carriages.		Kind of powder used.	Number of friction tubes that failed.	Commenced firing.	Ceased firing.	Number of shots fired from this battery.
	1	2	3	4	5	6								Feet.	Inches.					
	13-inch Mortar, 1861. Iron bed.	13-inch Mortar, 1861. Iron bed.	13-inch Mortar, 1861, Iron bed.																	
First day,	61	59	61				shells	$13\frac{1}{2}$	7	45°	26	3200	slight		$3\frac{3}{4}$	No. 5. Hazard's, and Smith and Rand's.	8	9 a.m.	7 p.m	181
Second day,	34	33	34				"	"	"	"	"		strong				7	6.15 "	2 "	101
Total,	95	92	95														15			282

Battery Burnside.

Days on which the firing occurred.	Description of pieces and carriages in the battery. Number of shots fired from each piece each day, and during both days.						Kind of projectile.	Charge for piece in pounds.	Charge for shell in pounds.	Elevation.	Length of fuze in seconds.	Distance from fort in yards.	State of wind, which blew from right to left.	Recoil of carriages.		Kind of powder used.	Number of friction tubes that failed.	Commenced firing.	Ceased firing.	Number of shots fired from this battery.
	1	2	3	4	5	6								Feet.	Inches.					
	13-inch Mortar, 1861. Iron bed.															No. 5. Hazard's, and Smith and Rand's.				
First day and night,	81						shells	10½	7	45°	24	2750	slight		3		3	9.15 a.m.	7 p.m	81
Second day	74						"	"	"	"	"		strong				1	6.25 "	2 "	74
Total,	155																4			155

REMARK.—Fired once every twenty minutes during the night.

Battery Sherman.

Days on which the firing occurred.	Description of pieces and carriages in the battery. Number of shots fired from each piece each day, and during both days. 1	2	3	4	5	6	Kind of projectile.	Charge for piece in pounds.	Charge for shell in pounds.	Elevation.	Length of fuze in seconds.	Distance from fort in yards.	State of wind, which blew from right to left.	Recoil of carriages. Feet.	Inches.	Kind of powder used.	Number of friction tubes that failed.	Commenced firing.	Ceased firing.	Number of shots fired from this battery.
	13-inch mortar, 1861. Iron bed.	13-inch mortar, 1861. Iron bed.	13-inch mortar, 1861. Iron bed.																	
First day,	44	44	44				shells.	10	7	45°	24	2650	slight.		3	No. 5. Hazard's, and Smith and Rand's.	6	9,15 a.m.	7 p.m	132
Second day,	34	33	33				"	"	"	"	"		strong				5	6.20 "	2 "	100
Total,	78	77	77														11			232

REMARK.—One shell burst about twenty yards from the piece.

Battery Halleck.

Days on which the firing occurred.	Description of pieces and carriages in the battery. Number of shots fired from each piece each day, and during both days. 1	2	3	4	5	6	Kind of projectile.	Charge for piece in pounds.	Charge for shell in pounds.	Elevation.	Length of fuze in seconds	Distance from fort in yards.	State of wind, which blew from right to left.	Recoil of carriages. Feet.	Inches.	Kind of powder used.	Number of friction tubes that failed.	Commenced firing.	Ceased firing.	Number of shots fired from this battery.
	13-inch mortar, 1861. Iron bed.	13-inch mortar, 1861. Iron bed.																		
First day and night,	60	60					shells	11	8	55°	29	2,400	slight.		1	No. 5. Hazard's, and Smith and Rand's.	3	8.15 a.m.	7 p.m	120
Second day,	50	50					"	"	"	"	"		strong				1	6.15 "	2 "	100
Total,	110	110															4			220

REMARK.—Fired once every twenty minutes during the night.

Battery Totten.

Days on which the firing occurred.	Description of pieces and carriages in the battery. Number of shots fired from each piece each day, and during both days.						Kind of projectile.	Charge for piece in pounds.	Charge for shell in pounds.	Elevation.	Length of fuze in seconds.	Distance from fort in yards.	State of the wind, which blew from right to left.	Recoil of carriages.		Kind of powder used.	Number of friction tubes that failed.	Commenced firing.	Ceased firing.	Number of shots fired from this battery.
	1	2	3	4	5	6								Feet.	Inches.					
	10-inch Siege Mortar, 1861. Siege Mortar bed.	10-inch Siege Mortar, 1861. Siege Mortar bed.	10-inch Siege Mortar, 1861. Siege Mortar bed.	10-inch Siege Mortar, 1861. Siege Mortar bed.												No. 5. Hazzard's, and Smith and Rand's.				
First day and night,	83	83	82	82			shells	4½	3	45°	18½	1650	slight		6		3	9.15 a.m.	7 p.m	330
Second day,	65	65	64	64			"	"	"	"	"		strong				9	6.15 "	2 "	258
Total,	148	148	146	146													12			588

REMARK.—Fired once every twenty minutes during the night.

Battery Lyon.

Days on which the firing occurred.	Description of pieces and carriages in the battery. Number of shots fired from each piece each day, and during both days. 1	2	3	4	5	6	Kind of projectile.	Charge for piece in pounds.	Charge for shell in pounds.	Elevation.	Length of fuze in seconds.	Distance from fort in yards.	State of wind, which blew from right to left.	Recoil of carriage. Feet.	Recoil of carriage. Inches.	Kind of powder used.	Number of friction tubes that failed.	Commenced firing.	Ceased firing.	Number of shots fired from this battery.
	10-inch Columbiad, 1861. Iron carriage, front pintle.	10-inch Columbiad, 1861. Iron carriage, front pintle.	10 inch Columbiad, 1861. Iron carriage, front pintle.													No. 5. Hazards, and Smith and Rand's.				
First day,	40	97	3				shells	17	3	16°	23	3100	slight	5			10	8.20 a.m.	7 p.m	140
Second day,	60	60	61				"	"	"	"	"		strong				8	6.15 "	2 "	181
Total,	100	157	64														18			321

REMARKS.—No. 1 being fired with a charge of 19 lbs. of powder at an elevation of 20°, two bolts broke in the diagonal braces of the front transom of the chassis. It continued firing for five hours, when two other of the above bolts broke, and it ceased for the day. Bolts were replaced. Second day it fired uninterruptedly. No. 2. Two bolts broke in transom of chassis, and were replaced without seriously interrupting the firing. No. 3. First fire broke four bolts in transom and diagonal braces of chassis. Charge, 19 lbs.; elevation, 20°; Third fire dismounted gun, carriage and chassis. They were mounted and repaired by next morning, and the piece fired uninterruptedly. Improper pintles and crosses had been furnished. Rails of chassis kept sanded.

Battery Scott.

Days on which the firing occurred.	Description of pieces and carriages in the battery. Number of shots fired from each piece each day, and during both days. 1	2	3	4	5	6	Kind of projectile.	Charge for piece in pounds.	Charge for shell in pounds.	Elevation.	Length of fuze in seconds.	Distance from fort in yards.	State of the wind, which blew from right to left.	Recoil of carriages. Feet.	Recoil of carriages. Inches.	Kind of powder used.	Number of friction tubes that failed.	Commenced firing.	Ceased firing.	Number of shots fired from this battery.
	10-inch Columbiad, 1861. Iron carriage, front pintle.	10-inch Columbiad, 1861. Iron carriage, front pintle.	10-inch Columbiad, 1861. Iron carriage, front pintle.	8-inch Columbiad, chambered. Wooden carriage.																
First day,	1	1	1	179			shot	10-in. Col'd. 20		5°		1740	slight	Nos. 1, 2, and 3: 6; No. 4: 4		No. 5. Hazard's, and Smith and Rand's.	12	9½ a. m.	7 p.m	182
Second day,		100	100	119			"	8-in. Col'd. 10		"			strong				10	8½ "	2 "	319
Total,	1	101	101	298													22			501

REMARKS.—Nos. 1, 2, and 3 fired with a charge of 20 lbs. and an elevation of 5°. Chassis thrown off the pintles at first fire. Nos. 2 and 3 mounted during the night. Second day fired uninterruptedly. Improper pintles and crosses had been furnished. Rails of chassis kept sanded.

Battery Lincoln.

Days on which the firing occurred.	Description of pieces and carriages in the battery. Number of shots fired from each piece each day, and during both days.						Kind of projectile.	Charge for piece in pounds.	Charge for shell in pounds.	Elevation.	Length of fuze in seconds.	Distance from fort in yards.	State of the wind, which blew from right to left.	Recoil of carriages.		Kind of powder used.	Number of friction tubes that failed.	Commenced firing.	Ceased firing.	Number of shots fired from this battery.
	1	2	3	4	5	6								Feet.	Inches.					
	8-inch Columbiad, chambered. Wooden carriage.	8-inch Columbiad, chambered. Wooden carriage.	8-inch Columbiad, chambered. Wooden carriage.																	
First day,	82	82	82				shells	10	$1\frac{1}{2}$	17°	23	3045	slight	3		No. 5, Hazard's, and Smith and Rand's.	10	8.20 a.m.	7 p.m	246
Second day,	61	61	60				"	"	"	"	"		strong				9	6.15 "	2 "	182
Total,	143	143	142														19			428

REMARK.—Sabots were thrown from 75 to 300 yards from the piece; most of them broken into two pieces, some into three.

Battery McClellan.

Days on which the firing occurred.	Description of pieces and carriages in the battery. Number of shots fired from each piece each day, and during both days.						Kind of projectile.	Charge for piece in pounds.	Charge for shell in pounds.	Elevation.	Length of fuze in seconds.	Distance from fort in yards.	State of the wind, which blew from right to left.	Recoil of carriages.		Kind of powder used.	Number of friction tubes that failed.	Commenced firing.	Ceased firing.	Number of shots fired from this battery.
	1	2	3	4	5	6								Feet.	Inches.					
	42-pounder rifled James. Barbette carriage, wood.	42-pounder rifled James. Barbette carriage, wood.	32-pounder rifled James. Barbette carriage, wood.	32-pounder rifled James. Barbette carriage, wood.												No. 5. Hazard's, and Smith & Rand's. Musket powder for filling rifle shells.				
First day,	80	101	101	101			shot	42-	full	$4\frac{1}{2}$°		1650	slight	6			70	$9\frac{1}{2}$ a.m.		403
	20						shells	pdr. 8												
Second day,	4	5	90	88			shot	32-					strong							
	94	93	7	9			shells	pdr. 6									45			390
Total,	198	199	198	198													115			793

REMARKS.—One 32 pounder front sight was broken off by a shot the first day. The grooves were kept well cleaned by a scraper. Many of the shots from No. 3 turned end over end. The other pieces gave perfect satisfaction.

Battery Sigel.

Days on which the firing occurred.	Description of pieces and carriages in the battery. Number of shots fired from each piece each day, and during both days.						Kind of projectile.	Charge for piece in pounds.	Charge for shell in pounds.	Elevation.	Length of fuze in seconds.	Distance from fort in yards.	State of the wind, which blew from right to left.	Recoil of carriages.		Kind of powder used.	Number of friction tubes that failed.	Commenced firing.	Ceased firing.	Number of shots fired from this battery.
	1	2	3	4	5	6								Feet.	Inches.					
	24-pounder rifled James. Siege carriage.	30-pounder rifled Parrott. Siege carriage.	30-pounder rifled Parrott. Siege carriage.	30-pounder rifled Parrott. Siege carriage.	30-pounder rifled Parrott. Siege carriage.	30-pounder rifled Parrott. Siege carriage.														
First day and night,	133	30 103	30 103	30 104	30 103	30 104	shot shells	24-pd. 5	full	$4\frac{1}{2}°$	$5\frac{1}{4}$	1670		5		No. 5. Hazard's, and Smith & Rand's. Musket powder for filling rifle shells.	80	9.15 a.m.	7 p.m	800
Second day,	116	117	117	117	117	116	shells	30-pd. $3\frac{1}{4}$	"								40	6.15 "	2 "	700
Total,	249	250	250	251	250	250											120			

REMARK.—Fired once every twenty minutes during the night.

RECAPITULATION.

Number of guns bearing upon the fort,	20	Number of shots fired from the guns,	3543
" mortars " " " "	16	" " " " " mortars,	1732
Total number of pieces bearing upon the fort,	36	Total number of shots fired,	5275

APPENDIX E.

REPORT OF LIEUTENANT T. B. BROOKS, NEW YORK VOLUNTEER ENGINEERS, TO GENERAL GILLMORE.

CAMP OF THE VOLUNTEER ENGINEERS,
HILTON HEAD, S. C., *May 1st*, 1862.

GENERAL:

IN accordance with your instructions, I have carefully examined, since the bombardment on the 10th and 11th ult., the condition of the batteries erected on Tybee Island, Ga., for the reduction of Fort Pulaski, and have the honor to respectfully submit the following report on the same, with remarks and deductions of my own, which you kindly gave me permission to add.

I. MORTAR PLATFORMS.

For plans and dimensions see Plate IV.

The 13-inch mortar (1861 pattern) platforms used, may be described in general, as consisting, (1) of a flooring of three inch pitch pine plank, laid on ground well rammed and levelled ; (2) on this flooring was placed a timber structure varying in the different platforms, but similar to the rail platforms described and figured page 105 and Plate No. 8 of "Heavy Artillery." The chief difference was in the larger timbers used in our platforms, and in the fact that the centre sleeper or cross piece was always omitted, except in some instances, blocks between the rails were used; also as our platforms were decked small outside rails or stringers, to support the ends of the deck, plank had to be introduced. (3.) On this framework a decking of "uniform stuff" furnished by the ordnance department, or common three-inch plank, was placed perpendicular to the line of fire, and fastened down in most cases, by side-rails, with four bolts in each.

Pickets three inches square and three and a half feet long, were freely used to stay the platform.

Plates of iron four and a half feet long, four inches wide by one-half inch thick, inches, were fastened on each platform, on which the eccentric wheels of the mortar-beds rested.

How well this plan answered will appear from the following facts:

1. STANTON BATTERY.—(THREE 13-INCH MORTARS.)

Substructure: i. e., flooring and timbers. The mortar-beds standing where they were last fired, were all found level both ways; hence it is inferred that the substructure has not changed, except, perhaps, to settle uniformly, which could not be prevented. When the decking is removed, the exact condition can be ascertained.

Decking.—In each platform one or more planks at the front and rear, particularly the former, were raised up and supported by sand which had worked in between the decking and rails. Sometimes this amounted to three inches. About seven feet in length of the centre was level, being held down by the mortar-beds. The ends curving up in this manner gave the platforms the appearance of having been warped by the sun.

The wear on the plank from manœuvring the piece, is scarcely appreciable in either platform of this battery.

The decking of the third or left mortar has slid back bodily several inches, pressing the four rear pickets, driven to prevent this movement, back and out of plumb.

2. GRANT BATTERY.—(THREE 13-INCH MORTARS.)

Substructure. As in the case of the Stanton, no deviation from the level plain can be found in the mortar-bed, hence it is inferred the substructure is not injured.

Decking.—First mortar; decking much raised up in front, but none in rear, has not slid back, plank but little worn. Second mortar; decking curved up in front and rear, has not slid back. Third mortar; decking in same condition as the second.

3. BURNSIDE BATTERY.—(ONE 13-INCH MORTAR.)

This platform is apparently in as good condition as the day it was put down.

Sergeant J. E. Wilson, U. S. Engineers, commanded this battery during the bombardment. He took care to fire the mortar in different parts of the platform, thus distributing the pressure and wear. The mortar was run forward nearly to the front of the platform, and then fired a number of times without being run in battery, until the recoil had carried it nearly to the rear of the platform, &c.

4. SHERMAN BATTERY.—(THREE 13-INCH MORTARS.)

First or right platform. This was the only 13-inch mortar

platform made entirely of plank (Fig. 1, Plate IV.) It consisted of a flooring of three-inch plank like the others. On this was laid in the direction of the line of fire, instead of timbers, six three-inch plank twenty feet long, two being placed under each cheek of the mortar. On this was placed, as in the other cases, a decking which was fastened down with side rails, having four bolts through each, the whole being well picketed.

Present condition. The platform is level crosswise, but has settled down two and a half or three inches in the centre, lengthwise, presenting a concavity upward, like the others already described, but from a different cause. Here the longitudinal planks have bent, and the platform has settled unequally.

The second and third mortar platforms of this battery (Fig. 2, Plate IV.) are in the same condition as the corresponding numbers in the Grant, *i. e.*, decking has slid back and has raised up in front and rear.

It is proper here to observe that in the Sherman and Burnside batteries, the platforms rest on a blue clay or mud mixed with sand and shells, while in the others fine pure sand only is found.

5. HALLECK BATTERY.—(Two 13-inch Mortars.)

Both the platforms at this battery are like the Burnside, apparently uninjured.

6. TOTTEN BATTERY.—(Four 10-inch Mortars.)

These platforms, like the first of the Sherman, were built entirely of planks, only smaller and somewhat differently arranged (see Plate IV., Fig. 5).

The planks were three inches thick, one foot wide, and ten feet long; four were laid equidistant and perpendicular to the line of fire, being ten feet from outside to outside; these were covered with a decking or flooring of eight planks in juxtaposition, perpendicular to the first. On this the decking of uniform stuff eight feet long was laid, and fastened down as above mentioned, by side rails. A plank was set on edge against the rear of the platform, its top being level with the top of the platform, and held in position by four pickets driven behind it.

Effect of the firing.—The two left of these platforms were entirely disabled by the first day's firing, and the others were much injured. These two were repaired at night, and all were nearly useless at the time of the surrender of the fort, about two o'clock next day.

The platforms of this battery were rendered useless—first, by being shaken to pieces, more or less, the parts being separated from each other, and held so by sand; second, unequal settlement, by which the platforms were made uneven, and out of level; third, moving backwards, bodily pressing over the plank and pickets behind it, set up to prevent this motion; fourth, the deck planks were much worn from manœuvring the pieces with iron-shod handspikes, having square, sharp corners.

The plank platforms of this battery are not so strong as the plank platform of the Sherman battery, and are far more injured.

The following summary embraces the most important facts relating to the mortar platforms constructed on Tybee Island:

1. The new pattern (1861) 13-inch mortar, and the 10-inch siege mortar, require platforms of about the same strength. If any difference, the 10-inch requires the strongest; or, at least that the parts composing it be the best fastened together.

2. A platform built of plank alone, as above described and figured Figs. 1 and 5, Plate IV., will not stand the fire of 10 or 13-inch mortars.

3. A "rail platform," decked over and resting on a plank-floor, was not in the least injured, except in its decking.

4. Pickets, three and a half feet long, and well driven, will not prevent platforms, or their decking, from moving backward from the recoil.

5. That platform from which the mortar was fired in different positions, the Burnside, is least injured; although it was fired more than an average number of times. See Legend, Plate II.

6. Sand worked into, and tended to keep open horizontal joints in the platforms, *e. g.*, the front and rear deck plank.

7. The wear on the deck plank of the 13-inch mortar platforms, where the eccentrics of the mortar-beds rested and rolled on the iron plates, is scarcely appreciable.

8. Three-inch pitch pine planks, twelve inches wide, make as good decking as uniform plank prepared especially by the ordnance department.

9. The injury to deck planks, from the square sharp corners

of the iron-shod manœuvring handspikes is great, and will soon destroy them.

10. Side rails, well bolted down, the bolts extending into the timbers of the substructure, can only be depended upon to secure the decking.

11. It is important that the different parts of a platform be well fastened together by lock-joints, pins, and bolts, so as to make a unit.

12. The earth on which the Sherman and Burnside platforms rest, is a blue clay, or mud, mixed with sand. All the others are built on pure, fine, quartz sand.

From the above facts I infer, that the essential parts of a platform, from which it is intended to fire directly a large mortar an indefinite number of times, the platform resting on fine quartz (beach) sand, are—

First. A flooring of heavy plank, with an area equal to 130 square feet, laid perpendicular to the line of fire, level, the earth being well rammed.

Second. A frame work on this, consisting of two rails or stringers, on which the cheeks of the mortar bed may rest, and two cross-pieces, or sleepers, near the ends of the rails, and united to them by a lock-joint. (See Plate 21, Heavy Artillery.) The under-face of the cross-pieces must be the thickness of the flooring planks below the under-face of the rails, so that the flooring plank and the cross-pieces, when the frame is together, may rest on the same levelled surface. The rails should be twelve inches square, or of dimensions equivalent, and the sleepers or cross-pieces two-thirds this size.

Third. The platform to be well secured by pickets, as shown (Heavy Artillery, Plate 21). The earth to be filled in to the top of the timbers, and well rammed. These precautions will prevent lateral motion, but will not entirely prevent the movement to the rear.

For direct firing, no decking would be required; but for large mortars, having eccentric wheels on their beds, a broader rail than above mentioned, would be necessary. With it, the platform would be complete.

If a plank decking be added, the plank should be at least three inches thick, well seasoned, and carefully laid. Pitch pine is excellent material. To support the ends of the decking, two additional rails, of four by eight inches, or six by six inches stuff, must be placed outside of the large ones, and be locked and pinned to the cross-pieces. On the four rails, or stringers, the upper surfaces of which are accurately brought to the same level plane, the decking plank is laid. To hold the deck plank down, and prevent it from sliding back, side rails are used.

These rails should be made of three by five inch stuff, placed over the outside rails below, and fastened to them by bolts of half-inch iron, which extend through the side rails, deck plank, and well into the rail below. The bolts should be not less than ten inches long, and be driven not more than one foot apart. Similar bolts should be driven through the front and rear deck plank, into each stringer.

To prevent sand from working in between the stringers and the decking, a plank should be set on edge, front and rear, as was done in the Totten battery.

The above-described platform probably possesses considerable surplus strength; but this mass, if well fastened together, helps greatly to keep the platform level, which is very necessary to accurate firing, particularly with inexperienced artillerists.

MORTAR PLATFORMS DESCRIBED IN "ORDNANCE MANUAL" AND "HEAVY ARTILLERY."

1. A platform for "Siege Mortars" is described on page 51, "Ordnance Manual," as consisting of—

"Wood: 6 sleepers, 18 deck planks, 72 dowels."

"Iron: 12 eye-bolts."

2. Another, or perhaps the same "Platform for a Mortar," is described and figured on page 105 and Plates 8 and 21, "Heavy Artillery," thus:

"The mortar platform is composed of only half the number of sleepers and deck planks required for the gun or howitzer platform. It is laid level and the front and rear deck planks are connected by eye-bolts to every sleeper."

3. On pages 105 and 107 and Plate 21, "Heavy Artillery," is described:

"The rail platform for siege mortars, composed of three sleepers," laid perpendicular to the line of fire, "and two rails for the cheeks of the mortar bed to slide upon instead of deck plank" (the timbers being united by lock joints) "is very strong and easily constructed and laid," &c., &c., &c.

Dimensions, &c., of the rail platform.

3 sleepers	60 inches long,	$11\frac{1}{2}$ inches wide,	$8\frac{1}{2}$ inches thick.
2 rails	84 " "	10 " "	10 " "
14 stakes	48 " "	$3\frac{1}{2}$ " "	$3\frac{1}{2}$ " "

It is evident that neither of the first two described platforms, being made of uniform plank, as they are evidently intended to be, would have stood the recoil of either style of mortar used at Tybee one-half day.

The rail platform might have stood, but would probably have soon become useless from unequal settlement.

II. GUN PLATFORMS.

1st. James rifled 64 and 84-pounders (old 32 and 42-pounders) on barbette carriages.

McCLELLAN BATTERY.

The platforms, chassis, and carriages of this battery, seem to have been injured very little, if any, by the firing. The last shot fired from the battery dismounted the left 84-pounder, on account of a defect in the chassis.

Sand was used freely on the rails of the chassis during all the firing, the recoil under these circumstances being three and a half or four feet.

For such direct firing it would probably have been better to have given the rails of the chassis a steeper slope than was used here, which is the same as is given for a wide field of barbette fire, a very different case from ours. Less sand, or none, would then have been required, and the guns would have been less apt to dismount themselves.

2d. Parrott's rifled 30-pounders on siege carriages.

SIGEL BATTERY.

These platforms were composed of five sleepers; the centre three, on which the trail and wheels rest, being of four by eight inch stuff, and the outside ones of one and a fourth inch plank.

Dowelled uniform stuff and common three inch planks were used for decking. No side rails were used.

Condition. The planks are slightly worn where the wheels and trail of the carriages rested when the gun was fired. Also, the joints of two or three planks just under the trail, have opened from one-half inch to one inch.

This could have been partially remedied, by eye-bolts through the plank on which the trail rested; or better, by side rails fastened down with bolts, as in the mortar platforms.*

3d. The 10-inch columbiads mounted on wrought-iron carriages and chassis, with one or two exceptions, dismounted themselves the first shot fired.

The recoil seemed to lift up the front of the chassis of the pintle-block, and to cause it to slide back bodily, causing the traverse wheels to slip off the circles.

The difficulty seemed to be: 1st. Pintle-blocks intended for 42-pounders were used, the bolts (pintles) of which were not large enough to fill the holes in the chassis of the columbiad, no proper columbiad pintle-blocks being at hand. 2d. No rear prop to receive part of the shock of the recoil was attached to the chassis. 3d. The substructure was formed of three heavy timbers, laid in the direction of the line of fire, without any cross pieces of any kind under them, to distribute the pressure over a wider space, and thus prevent unequal settlement.† 4th. The plank on which the iron traverse circle was fastened, was of a soft timber; it should have been the best oak, and at least four inches thick.

III. REVETTING.

Four methods were used at Tybee:

1. *A stake and brush revetting*, made by driving stakes eight feet long and three inches in diameter, two feet into the ground, stakes being placed one foot apart and sloping three on one. This row of stakes was anchored at the top by a rail in front, extending into the bank at each end, and well fastened by pickets. Behind these stakes, small brush of different kinds of wood, having leaves on them, was packed, the earth of the parapet being built up at the same time. A facine was placed on top and picketed.

This revetting allowed the dry sand to run through, and failed chiefly on this account. If mud or clay had been laid up with the brush, this plan would probably have worked well for four or five feet in height.

* Side rails would, of course, be unsuitable for siege platforms, except for direct firing, as was the case referred to. Q. A. G.

† This cannot properly be assigned as cause why the pieces were dismounted at the first discharge, when the circles and platforms were exactly level. Q. A. G.

This style of revetting (*i. e.*, without the mud) was used on the breast height of the Beach Battery at Hilton Head, young pines or pine sprouts being used for filling.

It did not leak sand, and seemed to answer well.

2. A rough hurdle work like the above in every particular, except, in most cases, no anchoring at the top was used, and the brush was rudely woven between the stakes.

This plan also allowed the sand to run through, and in every instance where no anchoring was used at the top—the support depended upon, to hold up the revetting, being the hold of the upright stakes in the ground below—the revetting failed, by being more or less pushed over.

3. A sod revetting was used in the Lyon battery, made of rough sods—wall one foot thick, six feet high, and sloping 2 on 1. It was anchored thus:—at every two feet in height, a board the length of one side,* was built in the wall like a long stretcher. To this board strips were nailed, which run back in the bank perpendicular to the revetting. Pickets were driven through notches in this board, and the anchoring strip into the revetting and the bank.

The plan of the revetting (each gun) of this battery, was a rectangle, open to the rear, its longest axis being in the line of fire. The front corners were rounded off, giving the plan the form of a horseshoe.

4. Fascines put up in the usual manner were used in the Totten battery, the fascines being made and anchored with withes. It leaked the sand very little, but did not sustain the earth. Part of it came down the first day, and the whole was in very bad condition at the end of the fight.

The fascine revetting of the McClellan and Sigel batteries stood well, but the earth was of a much more favorable character than in any of the others, containing considerable loam, and filled with roots. It stood up in the traverse 4 feet high, perpendicular, without revetting.

From the above I believe the following rules should be observed in revetting under similar circumstances:

1. All revetting for mortar or gun batteries should have a slope of 2 on 1.

* The rectangular area excavated for each gun, and opened to the rear, is referred to here. Thick traverses were left between the guns. Q. A. G.

2. For sustaining sand, the revetting must be almost water-tight.

3. Anchoring at the top is absolutely necessary, to secure revetting, whatever be the material.

4. Anchoring pickets for fascines must be driven at least as far back into the bank, as the fascine is above the foot of the revetting, and the same rule observed in anchoring any revetting.

5. Tarred rope or wire should be used in this region, to make and anchor fascines.

6. Of the materials used, sod was found best, fascine properly anchored would be next, and the stake and brush put up with mud, last.

IV. SLOPE OF SAND ABOUT THE BATTERIES AFTER THE BOMBARDMENT.

The angle of slope of the parapets, traverses, sides of magazines, &c., was measured with a clineometer at 10 points, with the following results:

$30° + 36° + 32° + 31° + 34° + 36° + 33° + 32\frac{1}{2}° + 31° + 31\frac{1}{2}° = 327°$.—$327°$ divided by 10 gives $32°\ 42'$ or about $33°$ as the mean; equivalent to a slope of $1\frac{55}{100}$ base to $1\frac{00}{000}$ perpendicular, or about $1\frac{1}{2}$ to 1. This may be assumed to be the least slope that fine dry quartz sand will take, under the influence of heavy firing.

If this slope be terminated by a berm 1 foot wide, where it rests on revetting, no trouble will be experienced from running sand.

V. EMBRASURES.

The following facts were observed:—

LINCOLN BATTERY.

Three 8-inch columbiads, in casemates of timber covered with earth. The cheeks had all tumbled down. They were sod walls 1 foot thick; slope 5 on 1, fastened by pickets $3\frac{1}{2}$ feet long, driven diagonally into the bank. The elevation of each cheek was a triangle, base about 12 feet, and perpendicular 8 feet.

They fell down from simple pressure of the sand, made to act by the concussion of the pieces. But little moving effect was produced in the sand by the blast of the guns, which were fired at a very high angle of elevation.

SCOTT BATTERY.

The two left guns, one 8-inch and one 10-inch columbiad, only, were fired at this battery. Elevation small.

Here the moving effect of the blast of the piece was very marked. At about 12 M. on Friday, being the second day of the bombardment, a hole had been excavated in the sole of each embrasure, about 2½ feet deep, below the axis of the piece in its centre, and extending 5 feet from the muzzle of the guns.

To repair this, twenty-five or thirty sand bags were put in each, and covered up with sand.

In two hours after, when the firing had ceased, this sand was found blown off, and some of the bags considerably burned.

The fascines with which the cheeks of the embrasures were revetted were not burned, but were undermined and much injured.

SIGEL BATTERY.

1 24-p'dr. James, 5 30-p'dr. Parrott. *Embrasures.* Throat 1 foot 8 inches wide, 3 feet high, and splay 25°. Revetting of fascines. No covering to soles.

The blast of the pieces moved the earth of the sole but very little, and produced no effect whatever two feet from the muzzle of the pieces. The sand was blown away from the fascines forming the cheeks, and they were much blackened, but not burned or charred, and but little injured.

McCLELLAN BATTERY.

2 42 and 2 32-p'dr. James. *Embrasures.* Throat two feet wide and three feet high. Revetting of fascines. No covering to soles.

Blast of pieces took effect 2½ feet from muzzle, blowing away the earth for 9 inches deep, and injuring the revetting on the sides. These embrasures were rebuilt the first night, and must have been the next, had the firing continued.

Part of the fascines taken out at night, after the first day's firing, were found to be so much burned as to be unfit for use.

Capt. Rogers, 7th Connecticut Volunteers, who commanded the battery, thinks this burning was on account of the fascines being set on fire by cartridge bags, and not by the direct contact of the blast.

SUMMARY. *

1. The effects of the blast of the columbiads is great, and is to be guarded against by covering the sole of the embrasure with some substantial material. Rifled thirty-two and forty-two pounders (James' sixty and eighty-pounders), are next in their effects, and should also be covered. With Parrott's it is very little.

2. With increase of elevation in the piece, the effect of the blast is rapidly diminished.

3. For making fascines or gabions to be used about embrasures, small brush or twigs should not be used; leaves should be carefully removed, and wire only used in making and anchoring them.

4. The effect of the blast of the largest guns does not extend more than five and a half feet from the muzzle.

5. For direct firing, embrasures having a splay of 25°, or even less, can be used.

6. The blast of either guns or mortars has very little power to burn from direct contact.

I think that the best revetting for embrasures would be gabions filled with sand-bags, the sole being covered with fascines. (2.) Fascines well made, and placed with sand-bags piled up behind them, would answer well. (3.) Palmetto logs, cut five feet long, set in juxtaposition on end, two feet in the ground, the sole being covered with short cross-pieces of the same, the ends fitting shallow notches in the uprights.

VI. MAGAZINES.

The timber used for the frames, was four by eight inch scantling. The bents (frames) were usually eight feet wide, and five or three feet high, resting on mudsills of the same stuff, one un-

* In judging of the effects of the blast upon the embrasures constructed against Fort Pulaski, it must be remembered that they had a splay of but twenty-five degrees, that the cheeks were somewhat steeper than generally prescribed, and that the soles were approximately horizontal; also that the columbiads were fired at an elevation of four and a half to five degrees—the 10-inch, with twenty pounds, and the 8-inch with ten pounds of powder; the 80-pounder and 60-pounder, James, with charges of eight pounds and six pounds, respectively, at four and a half degrees elevation; the 45-pounder, James, with five pounds, at four degrees elevation, and the 30-pounder Parrott, with three and a quarter pounds ,at four degrees elevation. Q. A. G.

der each post. The bents were placed three feet apart horizontally, and were framed at the corners. (Fig. 1.)

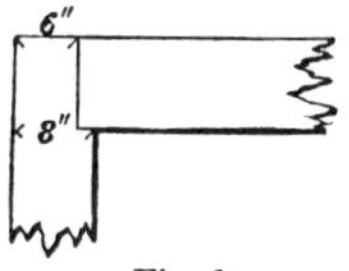

Fig. 1.

The sheathing and flooring were made of one and a quarter inch plank; two thicknesses being used on the top and one elsewhere. On this shell, seven feet of earth was placed, its sides sloping one on one and a half.

Entrances, with one and two doorways, were used, all so placed that if a shell burst outside, its fragments, moving in straight lines, could not reach the interior. Adjoining the magazine, the entrance was made five feet wide, to be used as a filling room for cartridges, and was arranged with shelves for cartridge bags.

The frames above described were not found strong enough, giving indications that they would fail by the breakage of the beams supporting the roof, and by the splitting of the shoulders of the posts on which the cross-timbers rested. Both difficulties were, in part, remedied, by placing an upright post in the centre of each bent, reducing the bearing of the cross-pieces supporting the roof to four feet, and relieving the vertical pressure on the side posts.

With this addition, none of the magazines failed, but there was evidently not surplus strength enough.

I think, had the bents, made of four by eight inch scantling, been placed two feet apart, instead of three, the centre post being retained, and a centre mudsill added to support the centre post (Fig. 2), and the proper mining joint (Fig. 3) substituted

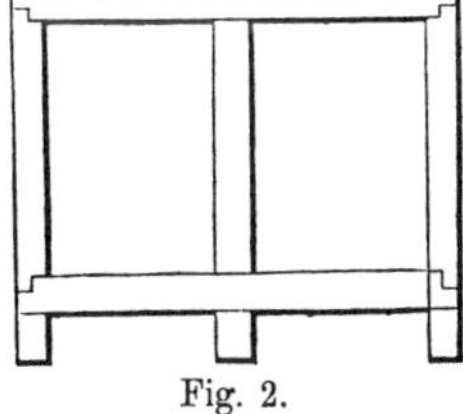
Fig. 2.

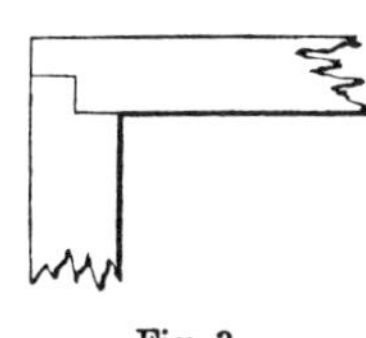
Fig. 3.

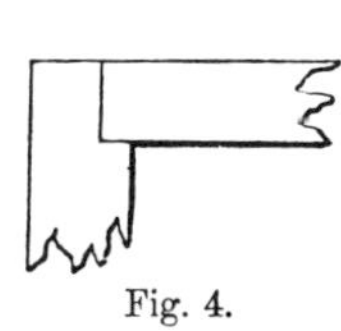
Fig. 4.

for the very defective one used (Fig. 4), no risk would have been run from the simple weight of the earth.

What effect a heavy mortar shell falling on such a structure, might have, was not experienced at Tybee.

The same difficulty was experienced in the magazines as in all structures where fine dry sand is exposed to the wind. It blew off very rapidly, thus not only diminishing the cover on the magazine, but filling up the covered ways, &c., &c. No permanency can be obtained except by sodding, or spreading over the surface a heavy coating of manure, which will cause grass and grain to grow.

VII. SPLINTER PROOFS.

Splinter proofs, in which the men forming the reliefs off duty might repose in comparative safety from the effects of shot and shell fired from guns, were built of pine logs, mud, and sand. Posts, four and a half feet long, were set in the ground, three feet apart, and of such slope as to be perpendicular to the rafters. On the top of these posts a longitudinal cap or plate was spiked. The rear revetting, about one foot high, was sustained by strong pickets, driven in the ground two feet, and standing two feet apart. It will be observed that the length of all the timbers used, and most of the dimensions of the splinter proof, are multiples of one and a half feet; the pickets being three feet, posts four and a half, and other pieces nine or eighteen feet. This fact simplified the cutting, hauling, and distribution of the timber greatly, part of which had to be done in the night. Only one kind of timber was got out in the woods, *i. e.*, pine trees, of from five to ten inches in diameter, cut into lengths of nine or eighteen feet, chiefly nine feet. It would have been better to have cut them off with a cross-cut saw. This stuff was delivered on the ground, at the rate of two nine feet pieces to the lineal foot to be built.

For posts it was cut once in two in the centre. For pickets, into three equal lengths, each of which made two or three strong pickets.

The rafters were laid in juxtaposition, the most prominent inequalities being hewn off to make better joints. Mud was plastered over the cracks, which made them completely sand-tight. Over this roof of timber three feet or more of sand was piled.

The longitudinal stick on top at the front edge of the rafters, to prevent the sand from running down in front, might advantageously be replaced by fascines or sand-bags.

Cross-traverses, of a double thickness of this uniform pine stuff, were placed at equal distances along one of the splinter

Plate X. Interior view of FORT PULASKI, showing method of protecting casemates with heavy square timbers.

Plate XI. BLAKELY 24 pounder rifle. 8 inch COLUMBIAD (dismounted) and Traverse.
Southeast face, looking towards Tybee.

proofs, intended to intercept fragments of shell, should one from a mortar fall through the roof and explode in one of the compartments. These would also serve to divide the space equitably among the occupants or reliefs.

One day's work of a soldier was found equal to covering an area of four square feet, including all the labor.

Hence to make two lineal feet, giving twelve square feet, which is sufficient for one man to lay down in with his arms, would require three days' work.

If the ditch in front be dug somewhat deeper than the floor of the interior, an excellent covered way is formed.

These structures should evidently be erected so high that the floors may be dry at all times, and should be placed out of the line of fire of the enemy's batteries; hence midway between our own batteries would be the safest place, if the batteries are near together, as at Goat's Point, Tybee Island. For cross-section of splinter-proof shelter, see Plate III.

I am, with great respect, your most obedient servant,

T. B. Brooks,
1st Lieut. N. Y. Vol. Eng'rs.

To Brig.-Gen. Q. A. Gillmore,
Commanding on Tybee and Cockspur Islands, Ga.

APPENDIX F.

RIFLE PROJECTILES.

Among the many kinds of rifle-projectiles called into notice and use by the recent wants of our service, are Parrott's, Schenkle's, Hotchkiss', James', and Sawyer's.

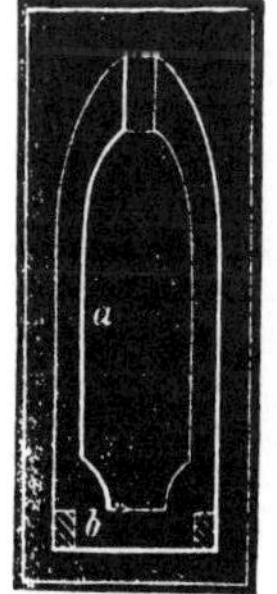

Fig. A.

*Parrott's.**—Parrott's projectile is composed of a cast-iron body (*a*) and a brass ring (*b*), cast into a rabate at the base of the body (see Fig. A).

The gas insinuates itself under the ring, forcing it into the rifles of the bore. In the smaller projectiles it is necessary to open the ring slightly for the entrance of the gas. Some of the projectiles used in Parrott's guns have a wrought-iron expanding cup attached to the base, constituting a modification of the Reed projectile.

* From Benton's Ordnance and Gunnery.

The iron cups do not possess any advantage over the brass ring.

Schenkle's.—Schenkle's projectile is shown in Fig. B. It is composed of a cast-iron body (*a*), the posterior portion of which terminates in a cone. The expanding portion is a *papier-mache* wad (*b*), which being forced forward on to the cone, is expanded into the rifling of the bore. On issuing from the bore the wad is blown to pieces, leaving the projectile entirely unincumbered in its flight through the air.

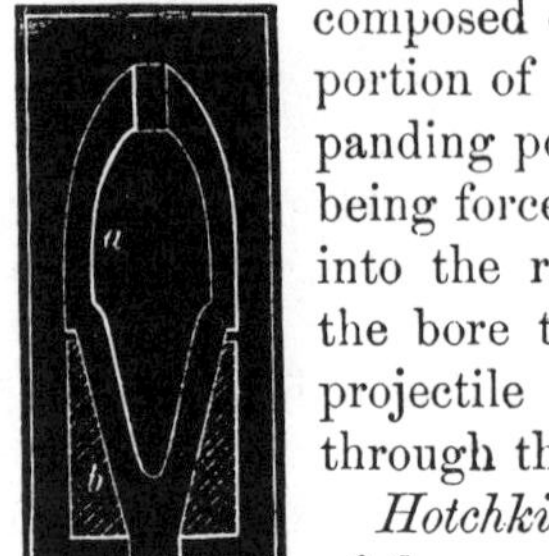

Fig. B.

Hotchkiss'.—Hotchkiss' projectile is composed of three parts, the body (*a*), the expanding ring of soft metal (*b*), and the cap (*c*), Fig. C. The action of the charge is to crowd the cap against the soft metal, thereby expanding it into the rifling of the bore.

Fig. C.

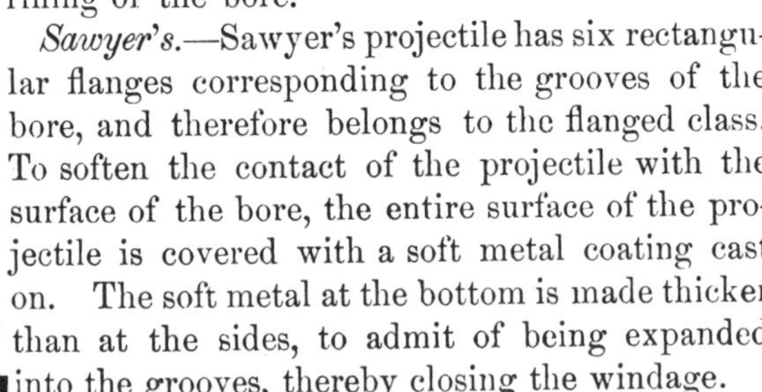

Sawyer's.—Sawyer's projectile has six rectangular flanges corresponding to the grooves of the bore, and therefore belongs to the flanged class. To soften the contact of the projectile with the surface of the bore, the entire surface of the projectile is covered with a soft metal coating cast on. The soft metal at the bottom is made thicker than at the sides, to admit of being expanded into the grooves, thereby closing the windage.

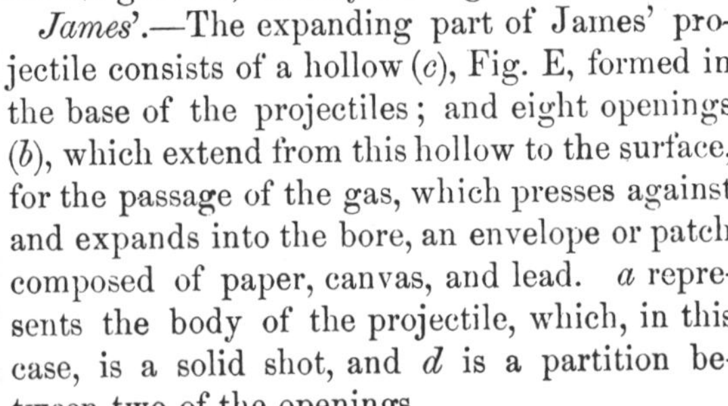

James'.—The expanding part of James' projectile consists of a hollow (*c*), Fig. E, formed in the base of the projectiles; and eight openings (*b*), which extend from this hollow to the surface, for the passage of the gas, which presses against and expands into the bore, an envelope or patch composed of paper, canvas, and lead. *a* represents the body of the projectile, which, in this case, is a solid shot, and *d* is a partition between two of the openings.

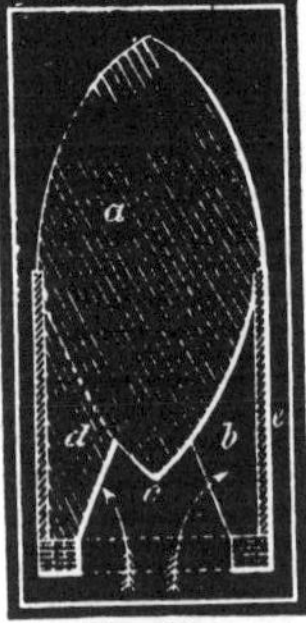

Fig. D.

Plate XII. 8 inch COLUMBIAD (piece broken out of muzzle) 10 inch COLUMBIAD (over the breach)
TRAVERSE railing around circular stairway 10 inch SEACOAST MORTAR dismounted (Southeast face).
Also blindages to casemates & inclined plane for serving ammunition to Barbette Guns.
Pieces all rendered unservicable during the first day's firing. View taken from the terre-plein of South face.

INDEX